It does not treat of minerals or fossils, of the virtues of plants, or the influence of planets; it does not meddle with forms of belief, or systems of philosophy, nor launch into the world of spiritual existences; but it makes familiar with the world of men and women, records their actions, assigns their motives, exhibits their whims, characterises their pursuits in all their singular and endless variety, ridicules their absurdities, exposes their inconsistencies, 'holds the mirror up to nature, and shows the very age and body of the time its form and pressure'; takes minutes of our dress, air, looks, words, thoughts, and actions; shows us what we are, and what we are not; plays the whole game of human life over before us, and by making us enlightened Spectators of its many-coloured scenes, enables us (if possible) to become tolerably reasonable agents in the one in which we have to perform a part. It is the best and most natural course of study.

– William Hazlitt, 'On the Periodical Essay', 1819

THE WILLIAM HAZLITT ESSAY PRIZE WINNERS 2013

–

Foreword by Harry Mount

Preface by Tom Kremer

Notting Hill Editions

Published in 2013
by Notting Hill Editions Ltd
Newcombe House, 45 Notting Hill Gate
London W11 3LQ

Designed by FLOK Design, Berlin, Germany
Typeset by CB editions, London

Printed and bound
by Memminger MedienCentrum, Memmingen, Germany

A CIP record for this book
is available from the British Library

ISBN 978-1-907903-88-5

www.nottinghilleditions.com

Contents

Harry Mount

– Foreword –

I've always thought the famous idiom about the elephant – it's hard to define but you know one when you see one – was brilliant, except that it didn't apply to elephants. They are in fact extremely easy to define – big, grey, large trunk, etc.

The idiom does apply, though, to the essay. Lots of people have tried to restrict it within the boundaries of a particular definition, but it never works. The only criterion, as far as I can tell, is quality, and even that's not a real criterion – a bad essay is still an essay.

But, like the elephant, you certainly know a good one when you see one. More than 700 essays were submitted for the 2013 William Hazlitt Essay Prize, covering a vast range of subjects. My notes on the principal subject of each essay show quite how vast: 'oyster . . . vole . . . lyric . . . Hereford . . .'.

I do hope the six essays that follow, chosen by all the judges, satisfy the elephantine criteria of a good essay.

Tom Kremer

– Preface –

The essay as a form is age-old, but also ageless. It may have originated in ideas of self-examination (Montaigne: 'it is many years since I have had only myself as the object of my thoughts') but is defined equally by its magpie capacity to inhabit any and every subject.

Its occasions are manifold: scholarly, journalistic, imaginative, personal. It can be linked to a fleeting moment or written with an eye to timelessness and universality. It can be factual, or it can float free of the evidence. The essay feels no obligation to have the last word. It can be as intricately crafted as a piece of marquetry, or it can exfoliate like a tree. This is very much in keeping with the English language, where the boundaries of word and meaning are loose, and the map of these boundaries continues to expand and change.

Given a plethora of definitions, however, it is sometime useful and necessary to move in a contrary sense, to redefine the reaches of a term. The 'essay' has had a long and adaptive history. In attempting to restore its specifically literary lustre, there is a case for contracting its boundaries, at a time when all non-fiction tends to borrow the name of 'essay'.

We should remember that the English essay possesses above all a personal impulse and an individual voice. It is not journalism, as such, nor is it scholarship as such. As one of the judges of the William Hazlitt Essay Prize has remarked: 'It is a form which balances the claims of intellect and emotion, or holds them in tension. This is its unique asset.'

In many ways the present is an opportune moment to return to the true meaning of essayism. At a time when words are tumbling, cascading, flooding over the printed or electronic page, filling newspapers, libraries and airwaves, the essay will survive and flourish – even if the book is under threat – because of its flexibility, but also on condition that it remembers its glorious past. As witness the winning entries in this competition.

Our publishing house, Notting Hill Editions, will always attend to what we believe to be the 'classical essay'. That is to say, a literary form expressing an original and universal idea in a language common to us all.

Michael Ignatieff

– Raphael Lemkin and Genocide –

If the history of the Western moral imagination is the story of an enduring and unending revolt against human cruelty, there are few more consequential figures than Raphael Lemkin and few whose achievements have been more totally ignored by the general public.

Lemkin coined the word 'genocide'. He was also its victim. Forty-nine members of his family, including his mother and father, were rounded up in eastern Poland and gassed in Treblinka in 1943. Lemkin escaped to America and in war-time Washington gave a name to Hitler's crimes in his monumental study of the jurisprudence of Nazi occupation, *Axis Rule in Occupied Europe*, published in 1944. He understood, earlier than almost anybody, that genocide was the darker purpose of Hitler's war: 'genocide is a new technique of occupation aimed at winning the peace even though the war itself is lost'.

After the war, thanks largely to his efforts, the UN approved the Genocide Convention and thanks to his crusade, by the early 1950s sufficient states had ratified the convention for it to enter into force. He never lived to see a conviction for the crime he was the first to name.

His campaign to promote the convention became an all-consuming obsession: he left adjunct posts at Yale and New York University, neglected himself, forgot to pay his rent, was evicted, went without food while spending all his days lobbying, cajoling, browbeating diplomats, politicians, public figures and newspapermen about genocide. Unfinished fragments of autobiography poignantly document his decline:

As I am devoting all my time to the Genocide Convention, I have no time to take a paying job, and consequently suffer fierce privations . . . Poverty and starvation. My health deteriorates. Living in hotels and furnished rooms. Destruction of my clothes. Increased number of ratifications . . . The labors of Sisyphus. I work in isolation, which protects me . . .

He collapsed at a bus stop on 42nd street in New York in August 1959 and died at the age of 59, friendless, penniless and alone, leaving behind a bare rented room, some clothes and a chaos of unsorted papers.

Donna-Lee Frieze, an Australian academic, spent four years in The New York Public Library, where the Lemkin material is deposited, reading faded typescripts, collating different drafts, deciphering illegible scribbles in ink and occasionally filling in gaps between or within sentences.

Now his autobiography has been published under Lemkin's chosen title, *Totally Unofficial*, a phrase from a *New York Times* editorial that praised him for what made his campaign unique: he did it purely as a private citizen, without foundation, academic or institutional support of any kind.

Lemkin belongs historically to a select list of humanitarians like Henri Dunant, who founded the Red Cross in 1863 and Eglantyne Jebb who created Save the Children after World War I, or going further back, to John Howard, the eighteenth-century sheriff of Bedfordshire who single-handedly awoke Europeans to the cruelty of their prison systems. These were all people who single-handedly changed the moral climate of their times by obsessional devotion to a private cause. Unlike Dunant, the wealthy son of Swiss merchants and Jebb, gifted daughter of a distinguished English landed family, Lemkin achieved what he did without the backing of private wealth: he was a penniless Polish refugee in America.

Donna-Lee Frieze has performed a labor of love with the materials Lemkin left behind but her best efforts cannot manage to turn the fragments into a complete and coherent book. Important chunks of the narrative are missing. We can only guess why Lemkin omitted to discuss his life between 1943 and 1945 when he worked in the Board of Economic Warfare in Washington and wrote *Axis Rule in Occupied Europe*, his unique study of the jurisprudence of genocide. Similarly missing is any treatment of his successful attempt to get genocide included in the official indictment of the Nazi war criminals at Nuremberg in 1945. Lemkin consigns these achievements to silence, leaving us to ponder his deeper motivations.

The final decline of lonely men is often a chronicle of self-delusion, persecution mania and paranoia. Lemkin's final years had its share of this, but it is also marked by aching awareness of the damage he was doing to himself. He appears to be one of Kafka's 'hunger artists', those moving, self-punishing creatures who cut themselves off from the world, preyed upon by a guilt they cannot name, who make their misery into their life's work. In some deep sense, Lemkin chose his own destruction and refused consolations that less complex characters would have easily embraced.

In his strangely lucid refusal of available consolations of career and company, he recalls another hunger artist of the same period, the young French philosopher Simone Weil. She starved herself so as not to eat more than the citizens of occupied Europe and died of tuberculosis at the age of 34 in a sanatorium in England in 1943, after completing what she called her 'war work' for the free French, a transcendent Declaration of the Duties of Mankind.[1]

Other pioneers in the battle to rebuild the European conscience after World War II – René Cassin who helped draft the Universal Declaration of Human Rights or Hersh Lauterpacht, who wrote the first treatise calling for an enforceable international convention on human rights – would have regarded these Jewish hunger artists with baffled pity. Cassin, from an assimilated and republican Jewish family in the south of France, joined De Gaulle's free French in London like Weil, but unlike her, never took it upon himself to suffer for others. Cassin went on to help draft the UN Declaration of Human Rights, and served as a judge on the European Court of Human Rights. He won the Nobel Prize for his work in 1968. Lauterpacht, a Polish Jew from the same region of eastern Poland as Lemkin, left before the killing began in the early 1920s, went to England and enjoyed a triumphant academic career, culminating in his appointment as Whewell Professor of Law at Cambridge and a term on the International Court of Justice. Like Lemkin, Lauterpacht watched helplessly from abroad as his entire Jewish family was destroyed in the Holocaust. Like Lemkin, he played an important role in the Nuremberg trials. Unlike Lemkin, he did not rage at Nuremberg's limitations and proved capable of working in a team, helping to write the briefs that Hartley Shawcross, the British prosecutor at the Nuremberg Tribunals, used to frame the indictment against the Nazi war criminals.[2]

As the Yale historian Jay Winter has argued in a fine recent study, both Cassin and Lauterpacht were Jewish insiders, while Lemkin remained an outsider, unmarried, untenured, unattached and ultimately alone.[3] His work on genocide finally became a trap from which he could not – and in the end did not wish to – escape.

His autobiography resists easy explanations as to why this should have been so. All one can see clearly is that he had a perverse genius for steering away from available safe harbors. He was a Jew who resisted full identification with his people, so he was never a part of any of the Jewish communities or organisations who might have taken him in; he was a proud Pole who kept apart from Polish communities in the United States; a legal scholar, too grimly obsessed with genocide to settle down with a stable academic career, though several beckoned, at Yale and at New York University; he was a human rights pioneer who quarreled with human rights advocates; he was a man who longed for company, but had no time for small talk; a man who, as he ruefully confessed, always wanted to avoid three things in life – 'to wear eye glasses, to lose my hair and to become a refugee'. Now all three things, he said, 'had come to me in implacable succession'.

From earliest childhood in Poland, he admitted to a peculiar fascination with tales of horror – the savagery of the Mongols, the cannibalistic rituals of primitive tribes, the brutal punishment Romans meted out to slave revolts. This obsession with human cruelty gave him the *raison d'être* of his life but it could only have deepened his crippling isolation.

One of the weirder and more poignant moments in his autobiography occurs when he meets a diminutive Chilean dancer in a half empty ballroom of the Casino in Montreux, Switzerland in 1948, while he was working on the Genocide Convention. After dancing with her ('she danced with an exquisite slant, her eyes

6

half closed') he spent the night bizarrely regaling her with gruesome stories of the cruelties meted out by the Spaniards to her Aztec ancestors.

This was a pattern. Potential friends drew away from him because his normal conversation was apt to dwell at unsavory length on horrible punishments and excruciating cruelties. He was a man who couldn't stop telling strangers his nightmares. He devoted every spare minute of his final years to a world history of genocide. This project, mad in its Borgesian determination to create a total encyclopedia of world cruelty, lay unfinished at his death.

It would be easy to turn aside from Lemkin's obsessions or dismiss them as sado-masochistic, were they not paired with a redeeming belief that fate had chosen him to save future generations from the genocidal furies that had claimed his own family.

The question that the autobiography raises but leaves unanswered is how he chose for himself the role of hunger artist. Extreme moral careers often have aesthetic roots: people choose their lives as dramatic acts of self-creation. There is something childlike, and also as unyielding as a child's desire, in Lemkin's self-dramatisation. From an early age, he imagined himself as a hero in the popular turn-of-the-century romantic novel, *Quo Vadis*, with its kitsch world of noble slaves and lasciviously corrupted Roman owners. At the height of his influence right after World War II, he struck the disabused and cynical diplomats at the UN as 'an agreeable fanatic' but by the end of his life, his self-dramatisation was a crippling caricature of lonely defiance, surrounded by imagined enemies bent on his humiliation and defeat.

Totally Unofficial, which he wrote in these final years, offered him an escape backward into his past. It is at its most alive when he evokes his childhood in the Jewish world of Eastern Europe before World War I. He was not from a *stetl* family or an Orthodox one, and while he went to Hebrew school, his culture was always Polish and Russian as well as Jewish, which helps to explain why, in his writings on genocide, he never isolated the Jews from the fate of others, insisting that the Nazis were as bent on the destruction of the Polish nation, as they were on the extermination of his own people.

His self-identification as a Jew was always relatively weak, and his objective was never to save the Jewish people from genocide but mankind as a whole. This is why, when other Jews who survived the Holocaust became Zionists and put their faith in a defensible state of their own, Lemkin put his faith instead in international law and a convention that would proscribe the crime forever for every victim group.

This does not mean he was not shaped, through and through, by Jewish fate, in his case, by the glory and the burden of being born a Jew in what the historian Timothy Snyder has taught us to call the Bloodlands, the killing fields of Byelorussia, Lithuania and eastern Poland. When Lemkin was born in 1900, these lands were the Pale of Settlement and under the rule of the Russian Czar. Jews were forbidden to own or farm land, to study in Russian cities or to trade in alcohol. Lemkin's father persisted as a small-holding farmer nonetheless and Lemkin remembered when the local Russian policeman arrived at the house on horseback, tied his horse to a tree and waited until Lemkin's mother and father came up with the bribe that would make him go away again.

When Lemkin was six, pogroms broke out in Bialystok, three miles away. While his family was never in danger, Lemkin remembered being told that the anti-Semitic mobs slit open the stomachs of some of their victims and stuffed them with feathers from pillows seized from their bedding.

From early in childhood, Lemkin learned to think of history as a bleak tale of torture and suffering. He writes, 'a line, red with blood, led from the Roman arena through the gallows of France to the pogrom of Bialystok'. Again, instead of seeing Jews as exemplary or unique victims of genocide, he placed their fate in the context of an unending cycle of human cruelty that was his mission to name and eradicate. So compelling was this mission that he was willing to endure almost any ridicule to accomplish it.

As a young law student in Germany in the 1920s, his heroes were two moral assassins. The first was the young Armenian who gunned down in the streets of

Berlin one of the Turkish pashas responsible for the Armenian massacres. The young Lemkin thrilled to the assassin's reported remark, as he watched his victim fall: 'This is for my mother.' The second assassin that kindled Lemkin's imagination was a Jewish tailor, Shalom Schwarzband, who also used a pistol, this time in the streets of Paris, to gun down Symon Petliura, a Ukrainian minister of war, whom he held responsible for the pogroms in the Ukraine that claimed the life of Schwarzband's parents. Both assassins were arrested, went to trial and were acquitted on grounds of insanity. Lemkin, still a student, wrote an article for a Polish magazine calling Schwarzband's act 'a beautiful crime'. The word beautiful tells us how strongly Lemkin's imagination was shaped by a romantic aesthetic of vengeance.

Vengeance contended with the law in the young lawyer's imagination, but the law finally won. Like the other young Jewish lawyers, Cassin and Lauterpacht, who came out of World War I determined to rein in the murderous propensities of the nation state, Lemkin held fast to a faith in international law that the brutal advance of Nazism and Communist dictatorship did nothing to dispel. He put his faith, first of all, in the League of Nations and the League's minority rights regimes. As Mark Mazower has shown, these were pioneering first attempts to ensure that national minorities in Eastern Europe would not fall prey to the vengeance of newly self-determining national majorities.[4]

The minority rights framework decisively shaped Lemkin's approach to genocide. Unlike Lauterpacht who came to see the individual as the primary subject requiring protection in international law, Lemkin remained wedded to the older League idea that it was groups who required protection from the murdering state. For Lemkin, the religious, ethnic and national group was the bearer of an individual's language, culture and self-understanding. To destroy the group was to destroy the individual. This vision helps to explain his otherwise inexplicable hostility to human rights, indeed his belief that Cassin's Universal Declaration, passed in the same year as the Genocide Convention, offered no protection against genocide.

Back in Warsaw in the 1920s after studies abroad, now working as a public prosecutor and building a prosperous private practice, Lemkin began to seek a role for himself beyond the confines of Poland. In 1933, working through the institutions of the League of Nations, Lemkin, then in his early thirties, proposed the adoption of two new international crimes of war – barbarity and vandalism – the destruction of collective groups and the destruction of cultural heritage. This contained the kernel of his vision of genocide.

He was just about to present these new ideas in person at a conference in Madrid when his proposals were denounced in a Polish paper for protecting Jews only and hence as unPolish. The head of the Polish delegation, Emil Rappoport, later a long-serving judge in Communist Poland, decided Lemkin should with-draw. This experience of anti-Semitism often sundered Jews' connection to their place of birth, but not in Lemkin's case. He always saw himself as a Pole, one reason, perhaps why today, at least since 2005, there is a plaque commemorating him on the site where his house once stood in Warsaw.

That house was bombed and destroyed when Ger-many declared war and invaded Poland in September 1939. The most vivid chapters of his autobiography describe the incredible odyssey of his escape. He survived a German dive-bombing attack on the train carrying him out of Warsaw and after eluding capture by the Russians, who invaded from the east, made his way on foot, along with thousands of other refugees, back to the still untouched Jewish villages of east-ern Poland. There for a few nights he lodged with a young Jewish baker and his family. Not for the first time, Lemkin was tormented by his inability to shake his own people awake to the dangers that lay in store for them. He asked the young baker whether he had heard of Hitler's *Mein Kampf* . Did he not know that Hitler had boasted he would kill the Jews like rats? The baker replied:

'How can Hitler destroy the Jews if he must trade with them? '

The baker had been under German occupation during the first war, in 1915. 'I sold bread to the Ger-mans; we baked for them from their flour. We Jews are an eternal people. We cannot be destroyed. We can only suffer.'

Lemkin sat with the baker's family through their Sabbath meal, that autumn night in 1939, watched the baker's wife with her 'air of solemnity, self-assurance and discreet kindliness' light the candles and joined them in the prayers, the deep serenity and dignity of the occasion shadowed by his own premonitory dread. Later that night, he heard the baker praying by himself in the next room, 'a crescendo of persuasion, solicitation, a delicate murmur of explanation'. From the next room, Lemkin listened to a dialogue with God, based in a covenant of deepest faith.

Next morning, however, the baker's son, a youth of about twenty, said bitterly that his parents' faith was inexplicable to him. 'They would all make marvelous corpses: disciplined, obedient, they would all move like one and die silently, in order and solemnity.'

It was only in 1945 at Nuremberg that Lemkin established for certain what had happened to his own family and to the baker's. There among the thousands of witness affidavits prepared for the trial of the Nazi war criminals, he found the one that described the final moments of the baker, his family and their village in 1942:

Without screaming or crying, these people undressed, stood around by families, kissed each other, said farewells and waited for the command of [the] SS Man who stood near the excavation [pit] with a whip in his hand . . .

Unable to rouse the baker to the danger ahead, unable even to persuade his own mother and father to leave their homes, Lemkin escaped to unoccupied Lithuania and then to Riga in Latvia. There he met the great historian of eastern European Jewry, Simon Dubnow. Two years later, Dubnow would be led to his death in the dark forests outside of Riga. His last words were 'Write it down! Write it down!'

From Riga, Lemkin secured an exit visa and flew to Stockholm, where scholars he had met in international law conferences in the 1930s gave him refuge and work at the university. There he persuaded officials in the Swedish government to get their consulates and businesses across Europe to send back the regulations, decrees and laws the Nazis were promulgating throughout their zones of occupation. Studying them in the Stockholm university library, Lemkin became almost the first legal scholar in safety abroad to detect the exterminatory logic behind Nazi jurisprudence: the dismissal of non-Aryans from all posts in occupied countries, the proscription of inter-racial marriage, the systematic destruction of Polish religious, cultural and social institutions, the proscription of the Jews, the regime of the yellow star, the creation of ghettos in Warsaw, Amsterdam and Lodz.

Believing he could only communicate what he had learned, if he could get himself to the United States, Lemkin contacted Malcolm McDermott, a Duke University law professor who had visited Lemkin in

Warsaw and had helped him translate and publish an English version of the Polish penal code. McDermott arranged an appointment for Lemkin at Duke, and armed with this letter, Lemkin secured a US visa. Even now Duke University, to judge by a recent visit of mine, seems barely aware of its historic role in enabling Lemkin's escape.

Lemkin's only available route to the US took him by plane from Stockholm to Moscow, then across Siberia by rail to Vladivostok, then by boat to Japan, followed by a Pacific crossing to Vancouver and Seattle, followed by a train journey that ended finally at Duke Station in Durham North Carolina in April 1941.

When McDermott met him and drove him around the city of Durham, 'a lively bustling city smelling of tobacco and human perspiration', full of people waving greetings to each other ('Hiya John', 'Hey Jack'), the exhausted Polish refugee could only burst into tears.

The America of spring and summer 1941 was still neutral, still observing the Nazi occupation of Europe from a safe distance. McDermott paraded Lemkin to audiences throughout North Carolina and neighboring states and everywhere he encountered genial, kindly incomprehension when he talked about the exterminatory intentions of the German regime.

This remained the case even after June 1941 when the Germans invaded Russia and the SS and their killing units began to scythe through the Jewish communities of eastern Poland. It was at Duke Station that he received a final letter from his parents, written on a scrap of paper inside a battered envelope, saying only 'We are well and happy that the letter will find you in America.' He dreamed of his mother – her eyes smiling through a mist of sorrow – and understood that his parents were doomed. Driving to yet another Chamber of Commerce talk in the byways of North Carolina, he shook his fist at the windscreen in helpless rage. He was, he wrote,

ashamed of my helplessness . . . a shame that has not left me to this day. Guilt without guilt is more destructive to us than justified guilt, because in the first case catharsis is impossible.

'Guilt without guilt': this phrase comes as close as the autobiography ever gets to explaining the self-lacerating obsession that gripped Lemkin until the end.

When America did enter the war after December 1941, he left Duke and went up to Washington to work in the Bureau of Economic Warfare. Even his boss, Colonel Archibald King, had trouble grasping that the German occupiers were not observing the 1907 Hague Regulations on Land Warfare. 'This is completely new to our constitutional thinking,' King said, when Lemkin tried to lay out Hitler's philosophy of occupation.

Lemkin wrote President Roosevelt urging him to issue a public condemnation of genocide in occupied Europe, but he hit the same wall of incomprehension

that Jan Karski, the envoy from the Polish underground, encountered when he met the President at the
White House in 1943, and later Felix Frankfurter at
the Supreme Court. It was Frankfurter who later said
of his meeting with Karski, 'I did not say he was lying.
I said I couldn't believe him.'

Lemkin was certainly the one person in Washington in 1943 who could have believed Karski, but the
two Poles never met. Unable to secure a hearing in
official Washington, Lemkin persuaded the Carnegie
Endowment for International Peace to fund and publish in late 1944 the work he had begun in Sweden on
the law of occupation under Nazi rule. It was in this
work that he gave what Winston Churchill had called a
'crime without a name' the name by which it has been
known ever since.

A frenetic, increasingly compulsive decade of activity followed, as Lemkin crisscrossed the Atlantic,
successfully arguing for the inclusion of the word –
genocide – in the Nuremberg indictments, and then
campaigning in Paris, London, New York and Washington for the passage of the Genocide Convention.
He took up residence in the corridors of the UN,
camping out in a delegates' lounge, a lonely, balding
refugee with an overstuffed briefcase, a fanatical mas-
tery of every comma in the convention draft and so
obsessively focused on genocide that diplomats came
to dread his approach.

It is typical of Lemkin's method that one decisive

breakthrough in his campaign occurred at one in the morning in a Geneva park when, unable to sleep, he accosted another insomniac, who happened to be the Canadian Ambassador, and persuaded him to arrange an appointment for Lemkin with the Australian President of the General Assembly in order to place the Genocide Convention on the UN's agenda. This was how he worked, cadging meetings and cajoling the powerful, until finally on December 10, 1948, the UN General Assembly, then meeting in Paris, passed the Convention. Instead of celebrating, Lemkin checked himself into a Paris hospital, suffering from exhaustion.

In retrospect, what seems extraordinary is that foreign ministers, diplomats and statesmen were willing to listen to him at all. He benefited from a very brief window of opportunity, when utopian plans for global order and global justice could get a hearing, when the war-time unity of the victorious allies had not yet collapsed into the acrimony of the Cold War. By 1948, the tide of commitment to justice for Nazi war crimes was ebbing. The British were already objecting to the Genocide Convention on the grounds that, surely, Nuremberg was enough. The Russians were becoming adamantly opposed to any inclusion of 'political groups' in the definition of genocide's victims. The Cold War was squeezing shut the narrow space in which the victorious super-powers could co-operate on projects of international legal reconstruction. By 1949, the UN Charter, the Universal Declaration of Human Rights, the Geneva Conventions and the Genocide Convention – the four basic pillars of the post-war legal order – had been erected. Lemkin could justly claim to have been responsible for one of them.

For the remainder of his life, he defended his definition of genocide against all comers, while extending it to cases, like the organised famine of the Ukrainian peasants, the Holodomor, that in those days were still awaiting recognition as genocidal crimes.

He was always indignant that genocide was associated solely with physical extermination, in whole or part of a group. He always believed that genocide could take non-exterminatory forms, as in the determined attempt he had seen in his native Poland to crush Polish language, culture and faith and turn a people into slaves.[5] That for him qualified as an attempt at genocide.

He would have been astonished and indignant at the after-life of his word – how, for example, victim groups of all kinds have pressed it into service to validate their victimisation and how powerful states have eschewed the word lest it entrain an obligation to act. The most shameful example of this came in 1994 when US authorities refused to use it during the killings in Rwanda in 1994 lest it trigger a legal obligation to intervene. He would have been dismayed that it took until Rwanda for an international tribunal to secure the first conviction under his convention.

We can only hope that his deepest conviction – that

genocide ran like a red thread through human history, past, present and future – is wrong. Hitler's dark appeal, Stalin's too, as well as the Khmer Rouge killers of Cambodia and the *genocidaires* of Rwanda, lay in offering their people a final solution: a world without enemies. Genocide is not murderous madness, but a politics that promises a utopia beyond politics: one people, one land, one truth.[6] Because genocide is a political utopia, it remains an enduring temptation in any society that resembles the Bloodlands of eastern Europe, those dark places where political authority will not allow minorities to live together without discrimination and hatred.

Lemkin did not live to see that the solution to genocide is not a convention in international law or a change in the dark hearts of men, but something simpler and easier to attain: democracy and freedom. Free societies, ones that allow differences to speak and be heard, that live by intermarriage, commerce, free migration, democratic societies that convert enemies into adversaries and reconcile differences without resort to violence, are societies in which the genocidal temptation is inconceivable.

The red thread can be snapped. We can awake from nightmare. We are not compelled to repeat and we are not required to become angels. We are simply required to live and let live, to embrace the minority competition of free societies. The solution to genocide lay closer to Lemkin than he ever realised: in the teeming streets of New York where he collapsed and died, in the wild and exuberant jostling of peoples and races that within several generations beyond his death became the new world we now take for granted.

The last word about him should be left to one of the minor characters in his autobiography, a person with a walk-on part who ends up haunting the story. It is the Chilean dancer at the Montreux Casino, who danced with him, with her eyes slanted, and then listened to him at the bar for hours afterwards as he shared his nightmares and his vision. When he finally stopped, she had one question: 'Do you really hope to stop this slaughter?' When he said he did, she looked at him strangely, 'like someone who was reaching into the beyond and said distinctly, "You will be a famous man after your death."' Now at last, perhaps, the dancer's prediction will come true.

NOTES

1   Simone Weil, *The Need for Roots: Prelude to a Declaration of the Duties of Mankind (L'Enracinement)*, London, Routledge, 1952.

2   See A. F. Vrdolak 'Human Rights and Genocide: The Work of Lauterpacht and Lemkin in Modern International Law', EJIL (2009), 20, 4, 1163–94.

3   Jay Winter, Antoine Prost, *René Cassin and Human Rights: From the Great War to the Universal Declaration*

(Cambridge, 2013); also 'Prophet Without Honors', *The Chronicle Review*, June 3, 2013.

4   Mark Mazower 'The Strange Triumph of Human Rights, 1933–1950', *Historical Journal* (2004), 47, 2, 379–98.

5   Dirk Moses 'Raphael Lemkin, Culture and the Concept of Genocide', http://fds.oup.com/www.oup.com/pdf/13/9780199232116.pdf.

6   On genocide as a utopia, see my 'Lemkin's Word', *New Republic*, 21 February 2001.

J. T. Barbarese

– Politics 2013 –

The neighborhood is bleak. These are narrow feeder streets, many split down the seams and waiting for new gas and water mains. Pipes stacked on sagged pavements, manhole covers flipped, broken glass on steps and what's left of the asphalt. On one corner a pile of sand, there for months, nobody knows why. On the opposite corner wrecked appliances short-dumped by whoever left the sand. Houses shuttered with plywood and sheet-metal. Couple bricked-up windows. Nobody knows who owns them.

There's a thirty-foot gap where two row houses used to stand – row-house fronts are fifteen feet wide. The one on the left caught fire. To get to it firemen had to break into the one on the right. Its owner was a woman who was in one of the Carolinas visiting her son, seeing her new grandbaby, back in a month. She had handed the key to her neighbor the fire-victim, but the key was on a hook in the burning house. So the firemen had to break into the absent woman's house to get to the roof and put out the fire. They left the door unsecured and windows broken. When the woman returned from Carolina a month later she found a wreckage of broken pipes, a ruptured soil line, frozen appliances, floors fouled with animal mess, and no electricity. Something dark-furred and smelly had been in her bed. The fire-victim was long gone, nobody knew where.

The woman collected the insurance and moved, probably to be with her son in Carolina, but nobody knows for sure. They tore down both houses.

—

It's a homely parish church. Granite exterior, ground level to pitched roof two stories above street-level, a chilly rosette over the entranceway, tasteful stained glass representations of gospel narratives. Inside, the Stations of the Cross are tucked into squat glass tents. The stone work looks medieval, the terrazzo floors bright and unspoiled.

Only the women among the parishioners seem fit to do any actual work. They enter in heavy plaid zipper jackets, ballooning sweaters with banded sleeves. The older women are wrapped in heavy wool scarves. They stand or kneel only if they can, and most can't. Flesh is piled on their limbs like slush. They waddle, limp, pivot, slouch, and collapse into pews that moan when they meet the wood. They wear sweats, rarely dresses. Some come in muumuus. Those not overweight or morbidly obese wear flannel shirts pulled over the waistbands of loose-fitting jeans.

The women possess a fearsome underclass chic. They not only worked for the clothes they wear but some of them ran the production line in the factory that shut down and moved overseas and disrupted a transition that saw one female generation follow the other like the seasons into the mill. The big sewing machines, the black looms, the long pressing tables, the clean hot smell of steamed cloth. Sweat and steam. They dressed a generation of prom kings and queens, altar boys and communicants (and even a few bar mitzvah boys) in cheap clothing that never wore out. Their kids and grandchildren wore the uniforms they made to Viet Nam and Grenada and got married in their tuxes.

Their fingers hang like chewed bamboo over the pews. They have less trouble kneeling because they are simply tougher than the men. While their sons and husbands were working out over a beef-with-double provolone at Nick's or selling swag out of trunks, they were raising kids, running looms, hanging clothes, taking rectal temperatures, cooking, screaming at each other on the front steps, sometimes battling with their fists. They mostly don't read – cataracts, illiteracy, undiagnosed dyslexia, attention spans exhausted from lifetimes of doing five things at once. Their mates fear them more than anything.

Some in their seventies look a decade younger than the male children hanging at their sides. Sight of them turns the heart in opposed directions. The women seem to have nosed something repulsive here. When they scan the crowd they skip the males, their eyes dulled by old constellations. They are disappointed in the way maleness has left the males. They want something new: the old, the really old, dignified oldness.

The men are dressed as if their mothers were still laying out their clothes. Thin and tubercular or alcoholic, pasty and paunched, guts over unbelted trousers (and an occasional monk's rope). Pants shiny in the seat from long hours on their own stoops arguing trades and firing butts at strays. Polo shirts open at the throat. Strange lines in the crotch. Occasional gold – fake – pendants, uniformly cruciform, which clip the pews when they rise or sit. Work shirts under nylon jackets with fake down stuffing. They kneel on artificial knees.

They look sick and out of season, as though undergoing bad pregnancies.

They shuffle in like little boys with bald spots, bad hearing, dentures, colostomy bags, gum disease, heart disease, circulatory disease. Some mope in the narthex between the holy water fonts and the poor box and religious literature tables trying to look their ages. They can't, they're too depressed. They were educated to see the world as lively but fallen and overseen, the metaphysical equivalent of the security state. Their self-consciousness was perfected through decades of erased expressions and Latin masses.

—

In the standard blue-collar neighborhood's model of church art, the artist represents tradesmen to tradesmen. Everything is subtly working class. The apostles in the low (concrete) reliefs making up the Stations of the Cross look like gym-rats after workouts, punchy, out of breath. There are too many grief-destroyed women averting their eyes – these Grays Ferry women look everything in the eye, and look it down until it's dead or it confesses – and other than a couple of beefy Romans with pecs modeled on the artist's favorite film actor or on local gangsters, little is memorable. Stripped and transfixed on the cross, girlish and disturbing, Jesus has strong features but for his mouth, which is F. Scott Fitzgerald's. ('Worrisome,' Hemingway called it.) The Virgin looks like the Blue Fairy in Pinocchio. Martha's bust-line is impressive. The Roman soldier wielding the flagella is Tony, who owns the corner candy store. Magdalene, stylishly hooded and svelte in a pink shawl, is a ringer for Melanie Griffith. All three women shade lowered eyes, touch pale unlined throats, and look off. They seem to be sharing a secret or about to giggle.

In mid-mass at the point where the sermon is delivered, the young priest walks to the lectern and reads announcements. He reads them badly. His voice is high and blunted by feedback. He syllabicates the names of the recently deceased and sounds like speech recognition software. In him the congregates see either the future of religion or a confirmation of the wisdom of clerical celibacy. Imagine, they think, if he had children. Picture the IQs.

—

On their deathbeds they will ask for the priest or the sacrament, whether they believe or not. They go to their final reward with food trays untouched, night stands overflowing with unread cards, sun-warmed pitchers of ice water and plants on the window sill. It all says, Life goes on. They receive the viaticum and die with the fabled tears of death in their eyes because they are seeing God, or God is watching as the morphine drip fills their arms and their sinus rhythms rise and fall on monitors down the hall. The girl on duty will be the granddaughter of somebody they grew up with or who died in one of the conflicts we no longer call wars, police actions or interventions. The girl will be sipping a 16-ounce diet drink while texting or talking to a boyfriend. She will remember, sort of, her own grandmother and for no reason think of a blurred erasure on a blackboard.

The luckier die at home. On their bed stands will be a cool water in a real glass, bifocals, a Band-Aid, wadded tissue, a rosary, a pencil stub and crossword puzzle. Family pictures, familiar furnishings, intense smells of the familiar – cooking, laundry, the family cat's litter box. A scapular will swing from the knob of the night table.

On the first floor on a muted wide screen the news and sports will be broadcasting what North Korea is doing, what the NFL or NHL is doing, what the fashion industry is doing, a consoling suite of self-canceling images.

On the first floor a daughter or daughter-in-law will be found bent over a counter, cooking or making a sandwich while listening to the radio. The family cat will enter dragging the scapular. Startled, she will glance at the cat, smile, make a friendly sound, turn back to her work and suddenly stop and look again at the cat, then wipe her hands and head up the steps, briskly.

—

On Mondays the girls and boys go back to school, the women back to their jobs, the men back to their stoops and firing cigarettes at strays. Many worked for one of the industries that existed when America's neighborhood economy was still industrial and it still made and exported things. There was the clothing factory that closed and relocated to a city in the southwest before it was again closed and relocated to Singapore or some other geographically desolate locale. There was the ice cream plant that closed a long time ago and didn't even relocate, just closed. There were other regional factories – locomotive boiler factories, jet engine plants – where some (too broke for cars let alone car insurance) bussed each morning, places where many worked as security guards, maintenance men, sweepers. All back in the day. The men like to say they're retired because it sounds better than unemployed, laid off, furloughed, riffed, living off an insurance scam, on disability, or fired.

—

They vote, pay taxes, tithe the church, and fly flags over their rotten awnings. They subscribe to the newspapers that pander to their interests and the politicians who pander to their needs. They find evolution ridiculous but find nothing strange about a man rising from the dead.

When the archbishop condemns abortion, they condemn politicians who disagree with the archbishop. Half of their kids had abortions and the other half paid for one. They all had kids and their kids have kids, often while they were still kids. They love babies, all babies are vital and innocent, there's no such thing as an unwanted pregnancy. Capital punishment is in the Bible. Where's it mention abortion? Where's it say 'evolution'?

You should keep what you earn, they say. Government is too big. Mostly jobless they blame joblessness on immigrants or liberals or Jews. They have stopped blaming the Blacks but still call them niggers just as they still call Jews kikes. It would be politically correct not to, and all they have left is their nostalgia for saying what's on your mind. Because that's what you do in America. You speak your mind. Who don't like it can move.

So they like reactionaries. Reactionaries say what's

on their minds. But not radicals, who are the liberals and the liberal media. They warm to appeals to frugality and fortitude in the face of the nation's decline and fall because they've seen lots of the former and are living the latter. They love how four (or is it five) members of the Supreme Court are Catholics. They love that there are two capos on the court (especially the one who compared Obamacare to broccoli). They see this as a triumph of the right kind of diversity. But diversity has its limits. The Founders were Christians, don't give us this church-and-state separation baloney.

They believe in a strict construction of the US Constitution. The right to bear arms is the right to bear arms. Same with Freedom of Speech (see above). Same with the Bible. It is what it says. Mostly, anyways. Jesus said turn the other cheek, forgive your enemy, but he was talking about the a-hole who pulls into the spot you just shoveled out or who snakes your girlfriend out from under. Had Jesus met these Ragheads with their suicide bombs and airplanes into buildings, He'd be singing a diffcrent tune, believe you me. Jesus, the first Neo-Con.

Mention Enron and they point to Ken Lay's dropping dead before trial. Evidence of God's existence. The mills of the Almighty.

—

They attend closely to Vatican successions. They were relieved when a cardinal named Joseph Ratzinger was elected pope since it's about time they gave a German the job. Best run country in the world. What we need now is a little colonel (wink-wink) to fix things here. If this new guy had grown up in the neighborhood, he would have been plain old Joey Rats.

When the pope quits they say, well, the man must be sick, a sick man, what, after all, in his eighties? Who would want that job? Somebody mentions a prophecy about the end-times and papal abdications but they ignore him.

When they elect the new pope they are relieved. A Jesuit, from South America somewheres. He's got a guinea name, he's Italian. He's an Italian raised in Argentina. His parents fled the Nazis? No, it was the Jews fled the Nazis, his parents were Nazis who fled the Allies. Anyway, we got the white smoke, one says. How long before he quits? They laugh. Who would want that job?

—

They hate politicians and love politics. Their parents were registered Democrats, so they register as Democrats, but after the Sixties and Nam and the race riots, their parents started to waffle, then came Nixon and they waffled more, and then came Reagan and their parents went Republican. So do they. Politics is what's in their freezer, whose kid got killed, who's got a job, who lost a house, how all the bankers ought to be hanged. They talk politics on the church steps, on the sidewalk, on their porches and stoops, on the bocce court at the playground, against the fenders of limos lined up for rides to Holy Cross, against railings, in taprooms where you best believe nobody is enforcing this no-smoking crap, at the corner body shop under the 25th Street Bridge, at booths at the Melrose (open 24 hours), or on line at the unemployment office where one guy turns to the one behind him (the women still have jobs) and asks Where'd you go to high school? because college was regular Army or, if you were cool, Marines. They grew up corner rats listening to the old guys at the pizza shop, which survived until a mob hit (they hit the wrong pizza shop) closed it. They ran prescriptions for the old Jew druggist until he moved to Florida, the drug store now owned by immigrants with pharmacology degrees and English so bad don't even dream of doing the prescription over the phone, you'll end up with poison. On the bakery steps two generations learned pinochle and some version of patriotism until it shut, after going from bakery to boutique to flower shop to hardware to video store, but its steps are intact. (Somebody on the block's grandfather poured the steps.) Afghanistan, Iraq I/II, and Grenada fade into outtakes from Nam, Korea, the South Pacific, the Bulge. They gather there – they still call it the bakery steps, right across from church – and talk war and do lines of dialogue from *Goodfellas*, *The Godfather*, *The Wire*. But deep dialogue, whole pages, How about them Japs bombing Pearl Harbor on Pop's Birthday?

or middle of a drought and the water commissioner drowns! It's how they spend their time. My parents used to sleep on their steps, they say. The Depression years, when air-conditioning was like sci-fi. My grand-mom scrubbed steps. Poor don't mean filthy.

Their despair is profound. It is a kind of wisdom.

Belle Boggs

– The Art of Waiting –

I t's spring when I realise that I may never have children, and around that time the thirteen-year cicadas return, burrowing out of neat, round holes in the ground to shed their larval shells, sprout wings, and fly to the treetops, filling the air with the sound of their singular purpose: reproduction. In the woods where I live, an area mostly protected from habitat destruction, the males' mating song, a vibrating, whooshing, endless hum, a sound at once faraway and up-close, makes me feel like I am living inside a seashell.

Near the river, where the song is louder, their discarded larval shells – translucent amber bodies, weightless and eerie – crunch underfoot on my daily walks. Across the river, in a nest constructed near the top of a tall, spindly pine, bald eagles take turns caring for two new eaglets. Baby turtles, baby snakes, and ducklings appear on the water. Under my parents' porch, three feral cats give birth in quick succession. And on the news, a miracle pregnancy: Jamani, an eleven-year-old female gorilla at the North Carolina Zoo, is expecting, the first gorilla pregnancy there in twenty-two years.

I visit my reproductive endocrinologist's office in May and notice, in the air surrounding the concrete and steel hospital complex, a strange absence of sound. There are no tall trees to catch the wind or harbor the now incessant cicadas, and on the pedestrian bridge from the parking deck everyone walks quickly, head down, intent on making their appointments. In the waiting room, I test the leaf surface of a potted ficus with my fingernail and am reassured to find that it is real: green, living.

The waiting room's magazine selection is scanty: a couple of years-old *New Yorker*s, the address labels torn off, and a thick volume of the alarmingly titled *Fertility and Sterility*. On the journal's cover, on a field of red, is a small, square photograph of an infant rhesus monkey clasped by unseen human hands in a white terry-cloth towel. The monkey wears a startled expression, its dark eyes wide, its mouth forming a tiny pink oval of surprise. A baby monkey hardly seems the thing to put in front of women struggling through the confusion and uncertainties of fertility treatment – *what are those mysterious, grayish blobs on the ultrasound, anyway?* – but, unsure how long I'll wait before my name is called, I reach for the journal. Flipping through, I find another photograph of the monkey and its monkey siblings, and the corresponding article about fertility preservation in human and nonhuman primates exposed to radiation. This monkey's mother, along with twenty other monkeys, was given an experimental drug and exposed to the same kind of radiation administered to women undergoing cancer treatment.

On other pages, I find research about mouse testicular cells, peritoneal adhesions in rats, and in vitro fertilisation of baboons.

Of course, this research was designed to study human, not animal, infertility. Nonhuman animals don't expose themselves to fertility-compromising radiation therapy, nor do they postpone reproduction, as I have, with years of birth control. Reproducing and ensuring the sexual maturity of offspring is a biological imperative for animals – their success depends on it, and in species after species we see that both males and females will sacrifice everything, their lives even, to achieve it. But in species with more complex reproductive systems – the animals genetically closest to humans – scientists have documented examples of infertility, hormonal imbalances, endometriosis, and even reproductive suppression. *How do they cope?* I wonder, staring at the photo of the baby rhesus monkey, its round, wide-set eyes designed to provoke a maternal response. Do they deal with infertility or the inability to become parents any better – or any differently – than we do?

My name is called, and a doctor I've never met performs a scan of my ovaries. I take notes in a blank book I've filled with four-leaf clovers found on my river walks: *Two follicles? Three? Chance of success 15–18 percent.*

On the way out, I steal the journal with the monkey on the cover. Back home, under the canopy of oak and hickory trees, I open the car door and sound rushes in, louder after its absence. Cicada song – thousands and thousands of males contracting their internal membranes so that each might find his mate. In Tennessee it gets so bad that a man calls 911 to complain because he thinks it's someone operating machinery.

—

A few days later, I visit the North Carolina Zoo, where Jamani, the pregnant gorilla, seems unaware of the dozens of extra visitors who have come to see her each day since the announcement of her condition. She shares an enclosure with Acacia, a socially dominant but somewhat petite sixteen-year-old female, and Nkosi, a twenty-year-old, 410-pound male. The breeding of captive lowland gorillas is managed by a Species Survival Plan that aims to ensure genetic diversity among captive members of a species. That means adult female gorillas are given birth control pills – the same kind humans take – until genetic testing recommends them for breeding with a male of the same species. Even after clearance, it can take months or years for captive gorillas to conceive. Some never do.

Humans have a long history of imposing various forms of birth control and reproductive technologies on animals, breeding some and sterilising others. In recent years, we've even administered advanced fertility treatments to endangered captive animals like giant pandas and lowland gorillas. These measures, both high- and low-tech, have come to feel as routine as the management of our own reproduction. We feel responsible when we spay and neuter our cats and dogs, proud when our local zoos release photos of baby animals born of luck and science.

Jamani and Acacia were both brought to the North Carolina Zoo in 2010, after Jamani was recommended for breeding with Nkosi, which was accomplished simply by housing the animals in the same enclosure. The zoo staff confirmed Jamani's pregnancy through an e.p.t. pregnancy test, the kind you can buy at a drugstore.

I ask Aaron Jesue, one of her keepers, if either Jamani or Acacia seem to have registered Jamani's pregnancy, if they've noticed any changes in behavior, but so far the only change is the increase in zoo visitors to the gorilla exhibit, and the many scientists and zookeepers they have consulted to help prepare for the birth. 'Jamani is still the submissive female,' Jesue says. 'We'll see if that stays the same.'

—

Many infertile women say that the worst part of the experience is the jealousy they feel toward pregnant women, who seem to be everywhere when you are trying (and failing) to conceive. At the infertility support group I attend, in the basement of another hospital an hour away, the topic of jealousy and petty hurts frequently begins our conversations.

'I don't mind babies and children, but I hate

pregnant women,' says one woman, trim and pretty, with a sensible brown bob. 'I hate them, and I don't care how that sounds.'

So we talk about that for a while: deleting Facebook friends whose frequent status updates document their gestational cycle, steering clear of baby showers and children's birthday parties. We talk about our fears that we will be left out, left behind, while our friends and relatives go about the business of raising their ever-growing families.

The family as a socially isolating unit is an idea not limited to humans. In the wild, infants represent competition for resources, and it is not uncommon for a mother's job to be primarily about hiding and protecting their infants from members of their own species. Jane Goodall observed chimpanzee mothers completely protecting their infants from contact with other nonsibling chimpanzees for the first five months of life, pulling their infants' hands away when they reached for nearby chimps.

In a marmoset community, the presence of a pregnant female can actually cause infertility in others, though the result is not isolation but rather increased cooperation. Marmosets are tiny South American monkeys that participate in reproductive suppression; that is, typically only one dominant female in a breeding group reproduces, often giving birth to litter after litter before any of the others has a chance. This is accomplished through behavior – some females simply do not mate – and also through a specialised neuroen-docrine response to the perception of subordination, which, like the pill, inhibits ovarian follicular devel-opment and ovulation. Some never get their chance, but remain in the submissive, nonbreeding category all their lives.

Marmosets are a mostly peaceful, cooperatively living animal. They make their nests in rainforest cano-pies and live in groups of three to fifteen, feeding on spiders, insects, and small vertebrates. Common mar-mosets are infrequently aggressive, with aggressive acts usually centering on the establishment of the breed-ing dominance of a female. Cooperation is remarkable among marmosets, particularly in regard to infant care. All group members over five months of age – male, fe-male, dominant, subordinate – participate, and a dom-inant female will allow her offspring to be carried by other group members from the first day of life. Scien-tists have speculated that this dependence on helpers – marmosets usually give birth to twins – is the reason for behavioral and hormonal reproductive suppres-sion. The phenomenon of suppression occurs both in the wild and in captivity.

Occasionally a subordinate female will reproduce, although her infant has a diminished chance of sur-vival. One reason is the practice of infanticide, which researchers have observed eight times in the wild (more frequently, the tiny infants just disappear). Infanticide most commonly occurs when a subordinate female gives birth during the pregnancy of the dominant female, who is often the attacker. Despite the apparent brutality of such a system, it does not seem to diminish social relationships or cooperation among the marmosets.

Sometimes cooperation is so extensive that it becomes difficult for researchers to establish which female is the biological mother. In one instance, recorded by Leslie Digby in Brazil in 1991, two adult females gave birth to twins in the same week. Less than a month later, two of the infants had disappeared, but because both mothers continued to nurse both surviving infants, it was impossible to tell which female was the biological mother or 'even whether those that disappeared were members of a single litter', according to Digby's report.

Like ours, the animal world is full of paradoxical examples of gentleness, brutality, and suffering, often performed in the service of reproduction. Female black widow spiders sometimes devour their partners after a complex and delicate mating dance. Bald eagle parents, who mate for life and share the responsibility of rearing young, will sometimes look on impassively as the stronger eaglet kills its sibling. At the end of their life cycle, after swimming thousands of miles in salt water, Pacific salmon swim up their natal, freshwater streams to spawn, while the fresh water decays their flesh. Animals will do whatever it takes to ensure reproductive success.

—

For humans, 'whatever it takes' has come to mean in vitro fertilisation (IVF), a procedure developed in the 1970s that involves the hormonal manipulation of a woman's cycle followed by the harvest and fertilisation of her eggs, which are transferred as embryos to her uterus. Nearly 4 million babies worldwide have been born through IVF, which has become a multibillion-dollar industry.

'Test-tube baby,' says another woman at the infertility support group, a young ER doctor who has given herself five at-home inseminations and is thinking of moving on to IVF. 'I really hate that term. It's a baby. That's all it is.' She has driven seventy miles to talk to seven other women about the stress and isolation of infertility.

In the clinics, they call what the doctors and lab technicians do ART – assisted reproductive technology – softening the idea of the test-tube baby, the lab-created human. Art is something human, social, nonthreatening. Art does not clone or copy, but creates. It is often described as priceless, timeless, healing. It is far from uncommon to spend large amounts of money on art. It's an investment.

All of these ideas soothe, whether we think them through or not, just as the experience of treating infertility, while often painful and undignified, soothes as well. For the woman, treating infertility is about nurturing her body, which will hopefully produce eggs and a rich uterine lining where a fertilised egg could implant. All of the actions she might take in a given month – abstaining from caffeine and alcohol, taking Clomid or Femara, injecting herself with Gonal-f or human chorionic gonadotropin, charting her temperature and cervical mucus on a specialised calendar – are essentially maternal, repetitive, and self-sacrificing. In online message boards, where women gather to talk about their Clomid cycles and inseminations and IVF cycles, a form of baby talk is used to discuss the organs and cells of the reproductive process. Ovarian follicles are 'follies', embryos are 'embies', and frozen embryos – the embryos not used in an IVF cycle, which are frozen for future tries – are 'snowbabies'. The frequent ultrasounds given to women in a treatment cycle, which monitor the growth of follicles and the endometrial lining, are not unlike the ultrasounds of pregnant women in the early stages of pregnancy. There is a wand, a screen, and something growing.

And always: something more to do, something else to try. It doesn't take long, in an ART clinic, to spend tens of thousands of dollars on tests, medicine, and procedures. When I began to wonder why I could not conceive, I said the most I would do was read a book and chart my temperature. My next limit was pills: I would take them, but no more than that. Next was intrauterine insemination, a relatively inexpensive and low-tech procedure that requires no sedation. Compared to the women in my support group, women who leave the room to give themselves injections in

the hospital bathroom, I'm a lightweight. Often during their discussions of medications and procedures I
have no idea what they're talking about, and part of
the reason I attend each month is to listen to their horror stories. I'm hoping to detach from the process, to
see what I could spare myself if I gave up.

But after three years of trying, it's hard to give up.
I know that it would be better for the planet if I did
(if infinitesimally so), better for me, in some ways, as a
writer. Certainly giving up makes financial sense. Years
ago, when I saw such decisions as black or white, right
or wrong, I would have felt it was selfish and wasteful
to spend thousands of dollars on unnecessary medical
procedures. Better, the twenty-two-year-old me would
have argued, to donate the money to an orphanage or
a children's hospital. Better to adopt.

The thirty-four-year-old me has careful but limited
savings, knows how difficult adoption is, and desper-
ately wants her body to work the way it is supposed to.

—

A large part of the pressure and frustration of infertility is the idea that fertility is normal, natural, and
healthy, while infertility is rare, unnatural, and means
something is wrong with you. It's not usually a problem you anticipate; from the time we are very young,
we are warned and promised that pregnancy will one
day happen. At my support group, someone always
says how surprised she is to be there.

My parents married in their early twenties and moved to the country to live on a farm and raise a family. It took them thirteen months to conceive me, and my mother says that during those months of waiting she thought she had been ruined by her previous years of birth control. That's how she put it – *ruined* – as if the rest of her working body, her strong back, her artist's hands, her quick wit, did not matter.

Although I married almost as young as my mother – I was twenty-six – it never occurred to me to have children right away. In my first year of marriage, I was teaching writing workshops to kindergarteners in Brooklyn, and at the beginning of the year I remember drawing and labeling a diagram of my bedroom on a big pad of paper while my students worked in their own notebooks. Daniel, a bright and charming five-year-old, pointed at the drawing of my bed – 'Why are there *two* pillows?' he asked. 'One for me, and one for my husband,' I said. He gasped. 'You're going to have a baby!' I laughed and shook my head. 'I'm too young to have a baby,' I said, though on parent-teacher night I realised that Daniel's own parents were younger than I was.

Three years later, I invited a public health nurse to speak to a group of fifth graders I was teaching in North Carolina. The subject of her talk was 'your changing bodies', a reliable source of giggles, but the nurse, a beautiful and soft-spoken woman who happened to be blind, brought a hushed seriousness to the talk. She angled her face upward so that her lecture took on the air of prayer, and she handled the plastic anatomical models of the vagina and uterus reverently. 'Your bodies are miracles,' she told the girls in a separate session. 'They are built to have babies. That is the reason for menstruation, the reason for the changes your body will go through.'

'Your brains are miracles, too,' I told them later. 'Bigger miracles than your uteruses. You don't have to have a baby if you don't want to.' But my words sounded feeble and undignified next to the nurse's serene pronouncement.

I'm always surprised when my students, boys and girls alike, from kindergarteners to high school seniors, talk about the children they will have someday. 'My kids won't act like that,' they say, watching an unruly class of kids on a field trip. Or, worriedly, 'I bet I'll have all boys. What will I do with all boys?' It seems far more common for them to imagine the children they might have than the jobs they might do or the places they might live.

Perhaps I shouldn't be surprised. Perhaps imagining ourselves as parents is not only the expression of a biological drive, but essential to understanding the scope of our lives, who we are and who we might become. For years I have dealt with a dread of old age and death by reminding myself that *I have not yet given birth*. I can imagine the moment clearly – my husband is there next to me, my parents are waiting to meet their grandchild – and the fact that it hasn't happened (always, it is at least nine months away) reassures me that some new stage of life is still to come. I'm not sure when people started asking me if I have children – a couple of years ago, I think. 'Not yet,' I always say.

Tillie Olsen's groundbreaking, feminist book *Silences* includes a chapter called 'The Damnation of Women' on the choice many women writers made between work and children. Olsen writes that it is not until the twentieth century that 'an anguish, a longing to have children, breaks into expression. In private diaries and letters only.' Her selections from Virginia Woolf's diaries in particular are extraordinary for their candor and pain. Woolf, who never had children, struggled with the idea of that loss for more than a decade, writing:

> . . . and all the devils came out – heavy black ones – to be 29 & unmarried – to be a failure – childless – insane too, no writer . . .

She seems to have conflated the failure to reproduce with a failure to write well, though she is only two years away from finishing her first novel. In her thirties, still childless, just a few years from writing *Mrs Dalloway*, she writes of 'having no children' and 'failing to write well' in the same sentence. At forty-four, she describes the dread she feels observing her sister's life as an artist and mother:

Let me watch the wave rise. I watch. Vanessa. Children. Failure. Yes. Failure. Failure. The wave rises.

It is only after embracing her writing as an 'anchor' that she makes peace with her childlessness:

I can dramatise myself as a parent, it is true. And perhaps I have killed the feeling instinctively; or perhaps nature does.

Because we spend much of our young lives dramatising and imagining ourselves as parents, it isn't surprising that even the strongest of us let the body's failure become how we define ourselves. But nature, which gives us other things to do, tells us otherwise. The feeling of grief subsides; we think through our options and make choices. We work, travel, find other ways to be successful. After completing *The Waves*, at forty-eight, Woolf writes of a feeling of intoxication that comes from writing well:

Children are nothing to this.

I'm no Virginia Woolf, but on occasion, after a good stretch of writing or time spent happily alone, I've had that feeling. It's thrilling, like taking a drug or riding a bicycle down a steep hill. Probably it isn't that different from the feeling a new mother has, looking at her child. *Not yet*, I've thought, suddenly protective of my time, my privacy, my freedom.

I once asked my father, 'Does having kids really squash all your dreams?'

He thought for a minute. 'Yep,' he said. 'And it takes all your money too.'

—

On the North Carolina Zoo's Facebook page, Jamani's keepers have posted a video of her latest sonogram. In a practiced pose, Jamani stands upright in an indoor room, clutching the steel grate that separates her from the zoo's staff. Her belly is accessible through a small gap in the grate. Humans and gorillas are so closely related that staff members wear hospital masks to protect themselves and Jamani from viruses.

'Hands up, hands up,' one zookeeper says, clicking a training noisemaker while another keeper feeds her from a platter of vegetables. 'Belly.' Jamani does not move her hands, but the keeper repeats the commands every few seconds. She is praised for her compliance, and the black-and-white image of her baby, looking not unlike the human sonograms I've seen on Facebook, appears on the veterinarian technician's laptop. I've watched it a dozen times, studying Jamani's face for clues to her comprehension.

So neat! comments one poster beneath the link.

She is doing great, says another.

The Baby is a cutie already, writes another.

Waiting in the outdoor enclosure during the filming, childless Acacia must be sitting on her haunches, chomping lettuce or carrots, oblivious to the fuss being made over Jamani, unaware of the fuss to come. Part of the reason for the attention from the media, from veterinarians, and from zoos across the country is the pregnancy's rarity among captive gorillas, and its uncertainty. In 2010, only six successful gorilla births were recorded in American zoos, and even when infants are born healthy, there's the chance that the mother will reject her young. If this happens, Jamani's keepers plan for Acacia to take over as a surrogate. Meanwhile, Acacia mates with Nkosi regularly though she has taken birth control pills since 2001 and will remain on birth control until the Gorilla Species Survival Plan determines that she is compatible with Nkosi. She may never conceive, but according to her keepers, she seems content.

Nonhuman animals wait without impatience, without a deadline, and I think that is the secret to their composure. Reproductively mature for more than half her life, Acacia waits without knowing she is waiting. The newly hatched cicadas will wait underground for another thirteen years. The submissive marmoset who declines sex, or whose ovaries fail to produce mature follicles, waits and waits – maybe forever.

Though infertile women are aware of the passing of months and years – marked by charts, appointments, prescriptions, and pregnancy tests – we have something animals lack, which is the conscious possibility of a new purpose, a sense of self not tied to reproduction.

51

I think it comes on us eventually, as Woolf suggests, but perhaps knowing that it comes, and understanding infertility as a natural, perhaps even useful phenomenon, can provide us with a measure of peace. Marmoset communities would not survive without their reproductively suppressed, caretaking females. Had Virginia Woolf been a mother, she may not have given us *Mrs Dalloway*, *To the Lighthouse*, *A Room of One's Own*, *The Waves*.

The cicadas stop their noise at the end of May. The adults are dead – eaten by other animals, worn out from their reproductive frenzy – and their wings litter the ground that will protect and nurture their young.

The silence is startling at first – I step outside each morning expecting to hear that seashell sound – but it's also a relief. I wait for some other wave.

POSTSCRIPT: *Jamani, expected to give birth in August, lost her infant to stillbirth in late June. Her keepers closed her exhibit to visitors and allowed her to hold and carry the baby until she made peace with the loss. Jamani did not allow Nkosi or Acacia to get close to the infant, but spent the day holding it, cleaning it, and trying to stimulate movement and feeding. Eventually, she set the infant down and walked away, signaling that she had grieved enough.*

Leslie Jamison

– The Empathy Exams –

M y job title is Medical Actor, which means I play sick. I get paid by the hour. Medical students guess my maladies. I'm called a Standardised Patient, which means I act toward the norms of my disorders. I'm standardised-lingo SP for short. I'm fluent in the symptoms of preeclampsia and asthma and appendicitis. I play a mom whose baby has blue lips.

Medical acting works like this: you get a ten page script and a paper gown. You get $13.50 an hour. Our scripts outline what's wrong with us – not just what hurts but how to express it. They dig deep into our fictive lives: the ages of our children and the diseases of our parents, the names of our husbands' real-estate and graphic-design firms, the amount of weight we've lost in the past year, the amount of alcohol we drink each week.

My specialty case is Stephanie Phillips, a twenty-three-year-old who suffers from something called conversion disorder. She is grieving the death of her brother, and her grief has sublimated into seizures. Her disorder is news to me. I didn't know you could seize from sadness. She's not supposed to know either. She's not supposed to think the seizures have anything to do with what she's lost.

STEPHANIE PHILLIPS
Psychiatry
SP Training Materials

CASE SUMMARY: You are a 23-year-old female patient experiencing seizures with no identifiable neurological origin. You can't remember your seizures but are told you froth at the mouth and yell obscenities. The seizures began two years ago, shortly after your older brother drowned in the river just south of the Bennington Avenue Bridge. He was swimming drunk after a football tailgate. You and he worked at the same miniature golf course. These days you don't work at all. You're afraid of having a seizure in public. No doctor has been able to help you. Your brother's name was Will.

MEDICATION HISTORY: You are not taking any medications. You've never taken antidepressants. You've never thought you needed them.

MEDICAL HISTORY: Your health has never caused you any trouble. You've never had anything worse than a broken arm. Will was there when it was broken. He was the one who called the paramedics and kept you calm until they came.

Our simulated exams take place in three suites of purpose-built rooms. Each room is fitted with an examination table and a surveillance camera. We test medical students in topical rotations: Pediatrics, Surgery, Psychiatry. On any given day of exams, each student must go through 'encounters' with three or four actors playing different cases.

A student might have to palpate a woman's ten-on-scale-of-ten-pain in her lower abdomen, then sit across from a delusional young lawyer and tell him that when he feels a writhing mass of worms in his small intestine, the feeling is probably coming from somewhere else. Then this med student might arrive in my room, stay straight-faced and tell me that I might go into premature labor to deliver the pillow strapped to my belly, or nod solemnly as I express concern about my ailing plastic baby: 'He's just so quiet.'

Once the fifteen-minute encounter has finished, the student leaves the room and I fill out an evaluation. The first part is a checklist: which crucial pieces of information did he/she manage to elicit? The second part of the evaluation covers affect. Checklist item 31 is generally acknowledged as the most important category: 'Voiced empathy for my situation/problem.' We are instructed about the importance of this first word, *voiced*. It's not enough for someone to have a sympathetic manner or use a caring tone of voice. The students have to say the right words to get credit for compassion.

We SP's are given our own suite for preparation and decompression. We gather in clusters: old men in crinkling blue robes, MFA graduates in boots too cool for our paper gowns, local teenagers in sweatpants. We help each other strap pillows around our waists. We hand off infant dolls. Little pneumonic baby Doug, swaddled in a cheap cotton blanket, is passed from girl

to girl like a relay baton. Our ranks are full of com-
munity-theater actors and undergrad drama majors
seeking stages, high-school kids earning booze money,
retired folks with spare time. I am a writer, which is to
say: I'm trying not to be broke.

We play a demographic menagerie: young jocks
with ACL injuries and business executives nursing
coke habits. STD Grandma has just cheated on her
husband of forty years and has a case of gonorrhea to
show for it. She hides behind her shame like a veil.
Her med student is supposed to part the curtain. If
he's asking the right questions, she'll have a simulated
crying breakdown halfway through the encounter.

Blackout Buddy gets makeup: a gash on his chin,
a black eye, and bruises smudged in green eye shadow
along his cheekbone. He's been in a minor car crash
he can't remember. Before the encounter, the actor
splashes booze on his body like cologne. He's supposed to let the particulars of his alcoholism glimmer
through, very 'unplanned', bits of a secret he's done his
best to keep guarded.

Our scripts are studded with moments of flourish: Pregnant Lila's husband is a yacht captain sailing
overseas in Croatia. Appendicitis Angela has a dead
guitarist uncle whose tour bus was hit by a tornado.
Many of our extended family members have died violent Midwestern deaths: mauled in tractor or grain-
elevator accidents, hit by drunk drivers on the way
home from Hy-Vee grocery stores, felled by a Big-10

tailgate – or, like my brother Will, by the aftermath of its debauchery.

Between encounters, we are given water, fruit, granola bars, and an endless supply of mints. We aren't supposed to exhaust the students with our bad breath and growling stomachs, the side effects of our actual bodies.

Some med students get nervous during our encounters. It's like an awkward date, except half of them are wearing platinum wedding bands. I want to tell them I'm more than just an unmarried woman faking seizures for pocket money. *I do things!* I want to tell them. *I'm probably going to write about this in an essay someday!* We make small talk about the rural Iowa farm town I'm supposed to be from. We each understand the other is inventing this small talk and we agree to respond to each other's inventions as genuine exposures of personality. We're holding the fiction between us like a jump rope.

One time a student forgets we are pretending and starts asking detailed questions about my fake home town – which it happens, if he's being honest, is his *real* home town – and his questions lie beyond the purview of my script, beyond what I can answer, because in truth I don't know much about the person I'm supposed to be or the place I'm supposed to be from. He's forgotten our contract. I bullshit harder, more heartily. *That park in Muscatine!* I say, slapping my knee like a grandpa. *I used to sled there as a kid.*

Other students are all business. They rattle through the clinical checklist for depression like a list of things they need to get at the grocery store: *sleep disturbances, changes in appetite, decreased concentration.* Some of them get irritated when I obey my script and refuse to make eye contact. They take my averted eyes as a challenge. They never stop seeking my gaze. Wrestling me into eye contact is the way they maintain power – forcing me to acknowledge their requisite display of care.

I grow accustomed to comments that feel aggressive in their formulaic insistence: *that must really be hard* [to have a dying baby], *that must really be hard* [to be afraid you'll have another seizure in the middle of the grocery store], *that must really be hard* [to carry in your uterus the bacterial evidence of cheating on your husband]. Why not say, *I couldn't even imagine?*

Other students seem to understand that empathy is always perched precariously between gift and invasion. They won't even press the stethoscope to my skin without asking if it's okay. They don't want to presume. Their stuttering unwittingly honors my privacy: *Can I . . . could I . . . would you mind if I – listened to your heart?* No, I tell them. I don't mind. Not minding is my job. Their humility is a kind of compassion in its own right. Humility means they ask questions, and questions mean they get answers, and answers mean they get points on the checklist: a point for finding out my mother takes Wellbutrin, a point for finding out my father died in a grain elevator when I was two – for realising that a root system of loss stretches radial and rhyzomatic under the entire territory of my life.

In this sense, empathy isn't just measured by Checklist Item 31 – *voiced empathy* – but by every item that gauges how thoroughly my experience has been imagined. Empathy isn't just remembering to say *that must be hard*, it's figuring out how to bring difficulty into the light so it can be seen at all. Empathy isn't just listening, it's asking the questions whose answers need to be listened to. It means acknowledging a horizon of context that extends beyond what you can see: an old woman's gonorrhea is connected to her guilt is connected to her marriage is connected to her children is connected to her childhood. All this is connected to her domestically stifled mother, in turn, and to her parents' unbroken marriage; maybe everything traces its roots to her very first period, how it shamed and thrilled her.

Empathy means realising no trauma has discrete edges. Trauma bleeds. Out of wounds and across boundaries. Sadness becomes a seizure. Empathy demands another kind of porousness in response. My Stephanie script is twelve pages long. There is so much it doesn't say.

Empathy comes from the Greek *Empatheia* – *em* (into) and *pathos* (feeling) – a penetration, a kind of travel. It suggests you enter another person's pain as you'd enter another country, through immigration and customs, border-crossing by way of query: *What grows where you are? What are the laws? What animals graze there?*

I've thought about Stephanie Phillips' seizures in terms of possession and privacy – that converting her sadness away from direct articulation is a way to keep it hers. Her refusal to make eye-contact, her unwillingness to explicate her inner life, the very fact that she becomes unconscious during her own expressions of grief, and doesn't remember them afterward – all of these might be a way to keep her loss pristine, unviolated by the sympathy of others.

'What do you call out during seizures?' one student asks.

'I don't know,' I say, and want to add, *but I mean all of it*.

I know that saying this would be against the rules. I'm playing a girl who keeps her sadness so subterranean she can't even see it herself. I can't give it away so easily.

LESLIE JAMISON
Ob-Gyn
SP Training Materials

CASE SUMMARY: You are a 25-year-old female seeking termination of your pregnancy. You have never been pregnant before. You are five-and-a-half weeks but have not experienced any bloating or cramping. You have experienced some fluctuations in mood but have been unable to determine whether these are due to being pregnant or knowing you are pregnant. You are not visibly upset about your pregnancy. Invisibly, you are not sure.

MEDICATION HISTORY: You are not taking any medications. This is why you got pregnant.

MEDICAL HISTORY: You've had several surgeries in the past but you don't mention them to your doctor because they don't seem relevant. You are about to have another surgery to correct your tachycardia, the excessive and irregular beating of your heart. Your mother has made you promise to mention this upcoming surgery in your termination consultation, even though you don't feel like discussing it. She wants the doctor to know about your heart condition in case it affects the way he ends your pregnancy, or the way he keeps you sedated while he does it.

I could tell you I got an abortion one February or heart surgery that March – like they were separate cases, unrelated scripts – but neither one of these accounts would be complete without the other. A single month knitted them together; each one a morning I woke up on an empty stomach and slid into a paper gown. One depended on a tiny vacuum, the other on a catheter that would ablate the tissue of my heart. *Ablate?* I asked the doctors. They explained that meant burning.

One procedure made me bleed and the other was nearly bloodless; one was my choice and the other wasn't; both made me feel – at once – the incredible frailty and capacity of my own body; both came in a bleak winter; both left me prostrate under the hands of men, and dependent on the care of a man I was just beginning to love.

Dave and I first kissed in a Maryland basement at three in the morning on our way to Newport News to canvass for Obama in 2008. We canvassed for an organising union called Unite Here. *Unite Here!* Years later, that poster hung above our bed. That first fall we walked along Connecticut beaches strewn with broken clam shells. We held hands against salt winds. We went to a hotel for the weekend and put so much bubble bath in our tub that the bubbles ran all over the floor. We took pictures of that. We took pictures of everything. We walked across Williamsburg in the rain to see a concert. We were writers in love. My boss used to imagine us curling up at night and taking inventories of each other's hearts. 'How did it make you feel to see that injured pigeon in the street today?' etc. And it's true: we once talked about seeing two crippled bunnies trying to mate on a patchy lawn – how sad it was, and moving.

We'd been in love about two months when I got pregnant. I saw the cross on the stick and called Dave and we wandered college quads in the bitter cold and talked about what we were going to do. I thought of the little fetus bundled inside my jacket with me and wondered – honestly *wondered* – if I felt attached to it yet. I wasn't sure. I remember not knowing what to say. I remember wanting a drink. I remember wanting Dave to be inside the choice with me but also feeling possessive of what was happening. I needed him to understand he would never live this choice like I was going to live it. This was the double blade of how I felt about anything that hurt: I wanted someone else to feel it with me, and also I wanted it entirely for myself.

We scheduled the abortion for a Friday and I found myself facing a week of ordinary days until it happened. I realised I was supposed to keep doing ordinary things. One afternoon, I holed up in the library and read a pregnancy memoir. The author described a pulsing fist of fear and loneliness inside her – a fist she'd carried her whole life, had numbed with drinking and sex – and explained how her pregnancy had replaced this fist with the tiny bud of her fetus, a moving life.

I sent Dave a text. I wanted to tell him about the fist of fear, the baby heart, how sad it felt to read about a woman changed by pregnancy when I knew I wouldn't be changed by mine – or at least, not like she'd been. I didn't hear anything back for hours. This bothered me. I felt guilt that I didn't feel more about the abortion; I felt pissed off at Dave for being elsewhere, for choosing not to do the tiniest thing when I was going to do the rest of it.

I felt the weight of expectation on every moment – the sense that the end of this pregnancy was something

I *should* feel sad about, the lurking fear that I never felt sad about what I was supposed to feel sad about, the knowledge that I'd gone through several funerals dry-eyed, the hunch that I had a parched interior life activated only by the need for constant affirmation, nothing more. I wanted Dave to guess what I needed at precisely the same time I needed it. I wanted him to imagine how much small signals of his presence might mean.

That night we roasted vegetables and ate them at my kitchen table. Weeks before, I'd covered that table with citrus fruits and fed our friends pills made from berries that made everything sweet: grapefruit tasted like candy, beer like chocolate, Shiraz like Manischewitz – everything, actually, tasted like Manischewitz.

Which is to say: that kitchen held the ghosts of countless days that felt easier than the one we were living now. We drank wine. I drank a lot of it. It sickened me to think I was doing something harmful to the fetus because that meant thinking of the fetus as harm-able, which made it feel more alive, which made me feel more selfish, woozy with cheap Cabernet and spoiling for a fight.

Feeling Dave's distance that day had made me realise how much I needed to feel he was as close to this pregnancy as I was – an impossible asymptote. But I thought he could at least bridge the gap between our days and bodies with a text. I told him so. Actually I probably sulked, waited for him to ask, and then told him so. *Guessing your feelings is like charming a cobra with a stethoscope*, a boyfriend told me once. Meaning what? Meaning that pain turned me venomous, that diagnosing me required a specialised kind of enchantment, that I flaunted feelings and withheld their origins at once.

Sitting with Dave, in my attic living room, my cobra hood was spread. 'I felt lonely today,' I told him. 'I wanted to hear from you.'

I'd be lying if I wrote that I remember what he said next. I don't. Not exactly. Which is the sad half-life of arguments – we usually remember our side better. I think he told me he'd been thinking of me all day, and couldn't I trust that? Why did I need proof?

Voiced concern for my situation / problem. Why did I need proof? I just did.

He said to me, 'I think you're making this up.'

This meaning what? My anger? My anger at him? Memory fumbles.

I didn't know what I felt, I told him. Couldn't he just trust that I felt something, and that I'd wanted something from him? I needed his empathy not just to comprehend the emotions I was describing, but to help me discover which emotions were actually there.

We were under a skylight under a moon. It was February beyond the glass. It was almost Valentines Day. I was curled into a cheap futon with crumbs in its creases, a piece of furniture that made me feel like I was still in college. This abortion was something adult.

I didn't feel like an adult inside of it.

I heard *making this up* as an accusation that I was inventing emotions I didn't have, but I think he was suggesting I'd mistranslated emotions that were already there – attaching long-standing feelings of need and insecurity to the particular event of this abortion; exaggerating what I felt in order to manipulate him into feeling bad. This accusation hurt not because it was entirely wrong but because it was partially right, and because it was leveled with such coldness. He was offering insight in order to defend himself, not to make me feel better.

But there was truth behind it. He understood my pain as something actual and constructed at once. He got that it was necessarily both – that my feelings were also made of the way I spoke them. When he told me I was making things up, he didn't mean I wasn't feeling anything. He meant that feeling something was never simply a state of submission but always, also, a process of construction. I see all this, looking back.

I also see that he could have been gentler with me. We could have been gentler with each other.

We went to Planned Parenthood on a freezing morning. We rummaged through a bin of free kids' books while I waited for my name to get called. We found a book called *Alexander*, about a boy who confesses all his misdeeds to his father by blaming them on an imaginary red-and-green striped horse. *Alexander was a pretty bad horse today.* Whatever we can't hold, we hang onto a hook that will hold it.

There are things I'd like to tell the version of myself who sat in the Planned Parenthood counseling room, the woman who studiously practiced cheerful unconcern. I would tell her she is going through something large and she shouldn't be afraid to confess its size, shouldn't be afraid she's 'making too big a deal of it.' She shouldn't be afraid of not feeling enough because the feelings will keep coming – different ones – for years. I would tell her that commonality doesn't inoculate against hurt. The fact of all those women in the waiting room, doing the same thing I was doing, didn't make it any easier.

I would tell myself: maybe your prior surgeries don't matter here, but maybe they do. Your broken jaw and your broken nose don't have anything to do with your pregnancy except they were both times you got broken into. Getting each one fixed meant getting broken into again. Getting your heart fixed will be another burglary, nothing taken except everything that gets burned away. Maybe every time you get into a paper gown you summon the ghosts of all the other times you got into a paper gown; maybe every time you slip down into that anesthetised dark it's the same dark you slipped into before. Maybe it's been waiting for you the whole time.

STEPHANIE PHILLIPS
Psychiatry
SP Training Materials (Cont.)

OPENING LINE: 'I'm having these seizures and no one knows why.'

PHYSICAL PRESENTATION AND TONE: You are wearing jeans and a sweatshirt, preferably stained or rumpled. At some point during the encounter, you might mention that you don't bother dressing nicely anymore because you rarely leave the house. It is essential that you avoid eye contact and keep your voice free of emotion during the encounter.

One of the hardest parts of playing Stephanie Phillips is nailing her affect – *la belle indifference*, a manner defined as the 'air of unconcern displayed by some patients toward their physical symptoms'. It is a common sign of conversion disorder, a front of indifference hiding 'physical symptoms [that] may relieve anxiety and result in secondary gains in the form of sympathy and attention given by others.' *La belle indifference* – outsourcing emotional content to physical expression – is a way of inviting empathy without asking for it. In this way, encounters with Stephanie present a sort of empathy limit case: the clinician must excavate a sadness that Stephanie can't fully experience herself.

For other cases, we are supposed to wear our anguish more openly – like a terrible, seething garment. My first time playing Appendicitis Angela, I'm told I manage 'just the right amount of pain'. I'm moaning in a fetal position and apparently doing it right. The doctors know how to respond. *I am sorry to hear that you are experiencing an excruciating pain in your abdomen,* one says. *It must be uncomfortable.*

Part of me has always craved a pain so visible – so irrefutable and physically inescapable – that everyone would have to notice. But my sadness about the abortion was never a convulsion. There was never a scene. No frothing at the mouth. I was almost relieved, three days after the procedure, when I started to hurt. It was worst at night, the cramping. But at least I knew what I felt. I wouldn't have to figure out how to explain it. Like Stephanie, who didn't talk about her grief because her seizures were already pronouncing it – slantwise, in a private language, but still – granting it substance and choreography.

STEPHANIE PHILLIPS
Psychiatry
SP Training Materials (Cont.)

ENCOUNTER DYNAMICS: You don't reveal personal details until prompted. You say you wouldn't call yourself happy. You say you wouldn't call yourself unhappy. You get sad some nights about your brother. You don't say so. You don't say you have a turtle who might outlive you, and a pair of green sneakers from your gig at the mini-golf course. You don't say you have a lot of memories of stacking putters. You say you have another brother, if asked, but you don't say he's not Will, because that's obvious – even if the truth of it still strikes you sometimes, hard. You are not sure these things matter. They are just facts. They are facts like the fact of dried spittle on your cheeks when you wake up on the couch and can't remember telling your mother to fuck herself. *Fuck you* is also what your arm says when it jerks so hard it might break into pieces. *Fuck you fuck you fuck you* until your jaw locks and nothing comes.

You live in a world underneath the words you are saying in this white room, *it's okay I'm okay I feel sad I guess*. You are blind in this other world. It's dark. Your seizures are how you move through it – thrashing and fumbling – feeling for what its walls are made of.

Your body wasn't anything special until it rebelled. Maybe you thought your thighs were fat or else you didn't, yet; maybe you had best friends who whispered secrets during sleepovers; maybe you had lots of boyfriends or else you were still waiting for the first one; maybe you liked unicorns when you were young or maybe you preferred regular horses. I imagine you in every possible direction, and then I cover my tracks and imagine you all over again. Sometimes I can't stand how much of you I don't know.

I hadn't planned to get heart surgery right after an abortion. I hadn't planned to get heart surgery at all. It came as a surprise that there was anything wrong. My pulse had been showing up high at the doctor's office. I was given a Holter Monitor – a small plastic box to wear around my neck, attached by sensors to my chest – that showed the doctors my heart wasn't beating right. The doctors diagnosed me with SVT – Super Ventricular Tachycardia – and said they thought there was an extra electrical node sending out extra signals – *beat, beat, beat* – when it wasn't supposed to.

They explained how to fix it: they'd make two slits in my skin, above my hips, and thread catheter wires all the way up to my heart. They would ablate bits of tissue until they managed to get rid of my tiny rogue beatbox and the pulse calmed back to normal.

My primary cardiologist was a small woman who moved quickly through the offices and hallways of her world. Let's call her Dr M. She spoke in a curt voice, always. The problem was never that her curtness meant anything – never that I took it personally – but rather that it meant nothing, that it wasn't personal at all.

My mother insisted I call Dr M to tell her I was having an abortion. What if there was something I needed to tell the doctors before they performed it? That was the reasoning. I put off the call until I couldn't put it off any longer. The thought of telling a near-stranger that I was having an abortion – over the phone, without being asked – seemed mortifying. It was like I'd be peeling off the bandage on a wound she hadn't asked to see.

When I finally got her on the phone, she sounded harried and impatient. Her voice was cold: 'And what do you want to know from me?'

I went blank. I hadn't known I'd wanted her to say, *I'm sorry to hear that,* until she didn't say it. But I had. I'd wanted her to say something. I started crying. I felt like a child. I felt like an idiot. Why was I crying now, when I hadn't cried before – not when I found out, not when I told Dave, not when I made the appointment or went to it?

'Well?' she asked.

I finally remembered my question: did the abortion doctor need to know anything about my tachycardia?

'No,' she said. 'Is that it?' Her voice was so incredibly blunt. I could only hear one thing in it: *Why are you making a fuss?* That was it. I felt simultaneously like I didn't feel enough and like I was making a big deal out of nothing – that maybe I was making a big deal out of nothing *because* I didn't feel enough, that my tears with Dr M were run-off from the other parts of the abortion I wasn't crying about. I had an insecurity that didn't know how to express itself; that could attach itself to tears or else their absence. *Alexander was a pretty bad horse today.* When of course the horse wasn't the problem. Dr M became a villain because my story didn't have one. It was the kind of pain that comes without a perpetrator. Everything was happening because of my body or because of a choice I'd made. I needed something from the world I didn't know how to ask for. I needed people – Dave, a doctor, anyone – to deliver my feelings back to me in a form that was legible. Which is a superlative kind of empathy to seek, or to supply: an empathy that re-articulates more clearly what it's shown.

During my winter of ministrations, I found myself constantly in the hands of doctors. It began with the nameless man who gave me an abortion the same morning he gave twenty other women their abortions. *Gave.* It's a funny word we use, as if it were a present. Once the procedure was done, I was wheeled into a dim room where a man with a long white beard gave me a cup of orange juice. He was like a kid's drawing of God. I remember resenting how he wouldn't give me any pain pills until I'd eaten a handful of crackers, but he was kind. His resistance was a kind of care.

Dr G was the doctor who performed my heart operation. He controlled the catheters from a remote computer. It looked like a spaceship flight cabin. He had a nimble voice and lanky arms and bushy white hair. I liked him. He was a straight talker. He came into the hospital room the day after my operation and explained why the procedure hadn't worked: they'd burned and burned, but they hadn't burned the right patch. They'd even cut through my arterial wall to keep looking. But then they'd stopped. Ablating more tissue risked dismantling my circuitry entirely.

Dr G said I could get the procedure again. I could authorise them to ablate more aggressively. The risk was that I'd come out of surgery with a pacemaker. He was very calm when he said this. He pointed at my chest: 'On someone thin,' he said. 'You'd be able to see the outlines of the box quite clearly.'

I pictured waking up from general anesthesia

to find a metal box above my ribs. I remember being struck by how the doctor had anticipated a question about the pacemaker I hadn't yet discovered in myself: How easily would I be able to forget it was there? I remember feeling grateful for the calmness in his voice and not offended by it. It didn't register as callousness. Instead of identifying with my panic – inhabiting my horror at the prospect of a pacemaker – he was helping me understand that even this, the barnacle of a false heart, would be okay. He offered assurance rather than empathy, or maybe his assurance was evidence of empathy, insofar as he understood that assurance, not identification, was what I needed most.

Empathy is a kind of care but it's not the only kind of care, and it's not always enough. I want to think that's what Dr G was thinking. I needed to look at him and see the opposite of my fear, not its echo.

Every time I met with Dr M, she began our encounters with a few perfunctory questions about my life – *What are you working on these days?* – and when she left the room to let me dress, I could hear her voice speaking into a tape recorder in the hallway: *Patient is a graduate student in English at Yale. Patient spent two years living in Iowa.* And then, without fail, at the next appointment, fresh from listening to her old tape, she bulleted a few questions: *How were those two years in Iowa? How's that PhD?*

It was a strange intimacy, almost embarrassing, to feel the mechanics of her method so palpable between us: *engage the patient, record the details, repeat.* I hated seeing the puppet strings; they felt unseemly – and without kindness in her voice, the mechanics meant nothing. They pretended we knew each other rather than acknowledging that we didn't. It's a tension intrinsic to the surgeon-patient relationship: it's invasive but not intimate.

Now I can imagine another kind of tape – a more naked, stuttering tape; a tape that messes up its dance steps:

Patient is here ~~for an abortion~~ for ~~a surgery to burn the bad parts of her heart for~~ a medication to fix her heart because the surgery failed. Patient is staying in the hospital for ~~one night three nights~~ five nights until we get this medication right. Patient ~~wonders if people can bring her booze in the hospital~~ likes to eat graham crackers from the nurse's station. Patient cannot be released until she runs on a treadmill and her heart prints a clean rhythm. Patient recently got an abortion but we don't understand why she wanted us to know that. Patient didn't ~~think she~~ hurt at first but then she did. Patient ~~failed to use protection and~~ failed to provide an adequate account of why she didn't use protection. ~~Patient had a lot of feelings. Partner of patient had the feeling she was making up a lot of feelings.~~ Partner of patient is supportive. Partner of patient is spotted in patient's hospital bed, repeatedly. Partner of patient is caught kissing patient. Partner of patient is charming.

Patient is ~~angry disappointed~~ angry her procedure failed. Patient does not want to be on medication. Patient wants to know if she can drink alcohol on this medication. She wants to know ~~if two bottles of wine a night is too many~~ if she can get away with a glass. Patient does not want to get another procedure if it means risking a pacemaker. Patient wants everyone to understand that this surgery ~~is~~ isn't a big deal; wants everyone to understand she is stupid for crying when everyone else on the ward is sicker than she is; wants everyone to understand her abortion is ~~also about~~ definitely not about the children her ex-boyfriends have had since she broke up with them. Patient wants everyone to understand ~~it wasn't a choice~~ it would have been easier if it hadn't been a choice. Patient understands it was her choice to drink while she was pregnant. She understands it was her choice to go to a bar with a little plastic box hanging from her neck, and get so drunk she messed up her heart graph. Patient is patients, which is to say she is multiple – mostly grateful but sometimes surly, sometimes full of self-pity. Patient ~~already understands~~ is trying hard to understand she needs to listen up if she wants to hear how everyone is caring for her.

I learned to rate Dave on how well he empathised with me. I was constantly poised above an invisible Checklist Item 31. I wanted him to hurt whenever I hurt, to feel as much as I felt. But it's exhausting to keep tabs on how much someone is feeling for you. It can make you forget that they feel too.

Dave doesn't believe in feeling bad just because someone else does. This isn't his notion of support. He believes in asking questions and steering clear of assumptions. He thinks imagining someone else's pain with too much certainty can be as damaging as failing to imagine it at all. He believes in staying strong enough to stick around. He stayed with me in the hospital, five nights in those crisp white beds, and he lay down with my monitor wires, colored strands carrying the electrical signature of my heart. I remember lying tangled with him, how much it meant – that he was willing to lie down in the mess of wires, to stay there with me.

I used to believe that hurting would make you more alive to the hurting of others. I used to believe in feeling bad because somebody else did. Now I'm not so sure of either. I know that being in the hospital made me selfish. Getting surgeries made me think mainly about whether I'd have to get another one. When bad things happened to other people, I imagined them happening to me. I didn't know if this was empathy or theft.

For example: one September, my brother woke up in a hotel room in Sweden and couldn't move half his face. He was diagnosed with something called Bell's Palsy. The doctors gave him a steroid called prednisone that made him sick. He threw up most days around twilight. He sent us a photo. It looked lonely and grainy. His face slumped. His pupil glistened in the flash, bright with the gel he had to put on his eye to keep it from drying out. He couldn't blink.

I found myself obsessed with his condition. I tried to imagine what it was like to move through the world with an unfamiliar face. I thought about what it would be like to wake up in the morning, in the groggy space where you've managed to forget things, to forget your whole life, and then snapping to, realising: *yes, this is how things are.* Checking the mirror: still there. I tried to imagine how you'd feel a little crushed, each time, coming out of dreams to another day of being awake with a face not quite your own.

I spent large portions of each day – pointless, fruitless spans of time – imagining how I would feel if my face was paralyzed too. I stole my brother's trauma and projected it onto myself like a magic-lantern pattern of light. I obsessed, and told myself this obsession was empathy. But it wasn't, quite. It was more like *in*pathy. I wasn't expatriating myself into another life so much as importing its problems into my own.

Jean Decety, a psychologist at the University of Chicago, uses fMRI scans to measure what happens when someone's brain responds to another person's pain. He shows test subjects images of painful situations (hand caught in scissors, foot under door) and compares these scans to what a brain looks like when its body is actually in pain. Decety has found that imagining the pain of others activates the same three areas (prefrontal cortex, anterior insula, anterior singulate) as experiencing pain itself. I feel heartened by that correspondence. But I also wonder what it's good for.

Whenever I woke up in the morning and checked my face for a fallen cheek, a drooping eye, a collapsed smile, I wasn't ministering to anyone. I wasn't feeling toward my brother so much as I was feeling toward a version of myself – a self that didn't exist but hypothetically shared his misfortune.

I wonder if my empathy has always been this, in every case: just a bout of self-pity projected onto someone else. Is this ultimately just solipsism? Adam Smith confesses in his *Theory of Moral Sentiments*: 'When we see a stroke aimed and just ready to fall upon the leg or arm of another person, we naturally shrink and draw back our own leg or our own arm.'

We care about ourselves and maybe some good comes from it. If I imagine myself fiercely into my brother's pain, I get some sense, perhaps, of what he might want or need, because I think, *I would want this. I would need this.* But it also seems like a fragile pretext, turning his misfortunes into an opportunity to indulge pet fears of my own devising.

I wonder which parts of my brain are lighting up when the med students ask me: *How does that make you feel?* Or which parts of their brains are glowing when I say, *the pain in my abdomen is a ten.* My condition isn't real. I know this. They know this. I'm simply going through the motions. They're simply going through the motions. But motions can be more than rote. They don't just express feeling; they can give birth to it.

Empathy isn't just something that happens to us – a meteor shower of synapses firing across the brain – it's also a choice we make: to pay attention, to extend ourselves. It's made of exertion, that dowdier cousin of impulse. Sometimes we care for another because we know we should, or because it's asked for, but this doesn't make our caring hollow. The act of choosing simply means we've committed ourselves to a set of behaviors greater than the sum of our individual inclinations: *I will listen to his sadness, even when I'm deep in my own.* To say, *going through the motions* – this isn't reduction so much as acknowledgment of effort – the labor, the *motions*, the dance – of getting inside another person's state of heart or mind.

This confession of effort chafes against the notion that empathy should always rise unbidden, that 'genuine' means the same thing as 'unwilled,' that intentionality is the enemy of love. But I believe in intention and I believe in work. I believe in waking up in the middle of the night and packing our bags and leaving our worst selves for our better ones.

LESLIE JAMISON
Ob-Gyn
SP Training Materials (Cont.)

OPENING LINE: You don't need one. Everyone comes here for the same reason.

PHYSICAL PRESENTATION AND TONE: Wear loose pants. You have been told to wear loose pants. Keep your voice steady and articulate. You are about to spread your legs for a doctor who doesn't know your name. You know the drill, sort of. Act like you do.

ENCOUNTER DYNAMICS: Answer every question like you're clarifying a coffee order. Be courteous. Nod vigorously. Make sure your heart stays on the other side of the white wall behind you. If the nurse asks you whether you are sure about getting the procedure, say *yes* without missing a beat. Say *yes* without a trace of doubt. Don't mention the way you felt when you first saw the pink cross on the stick – that sudden expansive joy at the possibility of a child, at your own capacity to have one. Don't mention this single moment of joy because it might make it seem as if you aren't completely sure about what you're about to do. Don't mention this single moment of joy because it might hurt. It will feel – more than anything else – like the measure of what you're giving up. It maps the edges of your voluntary loss.

Instead, tell the nurse you weren't using birth control but wasn't that silly and now you are going to start.

If she asks what forms of birth control you have used in the past, say condoms. Suddenly every guy you've ever slept with is in the room with you. Ignore them. Ignore the memory of that first time − all that fumbling, and then pain − while Rod Stewart crooned 'Broken Arrow' from a boombox on the dresser. *Who else is gonna bring you a broken arrow? Who else is gonna bring you a bottle of rain?*

Say you used condoms but don't think about all the times you didn't − in an Iowan graveyard, in a little car by a dark river − and definitely don't say why, how the risk made you feel close to those boys, how you courted the incredible gravity of what your bodies could do together.

If the nurse asks about your current partner, you should say, *we are very committed*, like you are defending yourself against some legal charge. If the nurse is listening closely, she should hear fear nestled like an egg inside your certainty.

If the nurse asks whether you drink, say yes to that too. Of course you do. Your lifestyle habits include drinking to excess. You do this even when you know there is a fetus inside you. You do it to forget there is a fetus inside you; or to feel like maybe this is just a movie about a fetus being inside you.

The nurse will eventually ask, *how do you feel about getting the procedure?* Tell her you feel sad but you know it's the right choice, because this seems like the right thing to say, even though it's a lie. You mainly feel numb. You feel numb until your legs are in the stirrups. Then you hurt. Whatever anesthesia comes through the needle in your arm only sedates you. Days later you feel your body cramping in the night − a deep, hot, twisting pain − and you can only lie still and hope it passes, beg for sleep, drink for sleep, resent Dave for sleeping next to you. You can only watch your body bleed like an inscrutable, stubborn object − something harmed and cumbersome and not entirely yours. You leave your body and don't come back for a month. You come back angry.

You wake up from another round of anesthesia and they tell you all their burning didn't burn away the part of your heart that was broken. You come back and find you aren't alone. You weren't alone when you were cramping through the night and you're not alone now. Dave spends every night in the hospital. You want to tell him how disgusting your body feels: your unwashed skin and greasy hair. You want him to listen, for hours if necessary, and feel everything exactly as you feel it – your pair of hearts in such synchronised rhythm any monitor would show it; your pair of hearts playing two crippled bunnies mating anyway. There is no end to this fantasy of closeness. *Who else is gonna bring you a broken arrow?* You want him to break with you. You want him to hurt in a womb he doesn't have; you want him to admit he can't hurt that way. You want him to know how it feels in every one of your nerve endings: lying prone on the detergent sheets, lifting your shirt for one more cardiac resident, one more stranger, letting him attach his clips to the line of hooks under your breast, letting him print out your heart, once more, to see if its rhythm has turned.

It all returns to this: you want him close to your damage. You want humility and presumption and whatever lies between, you want that too. You're tired of begging for it. You're tired of grading him on how well he gives it. You want to learn how to stop feeling sorry for yourself. You want to write an essay about the lesson. You throw away the checklist and let him climb into your hospital bed. You let him part the heart wires. You sleep. He sleeps. You wake, pulse feeling for another pulse, and there he is again.

Andrew O'Hagan

– Light Entertainment –

On 23 May 1949, Lionel Gamlin, producer of
the Light Programme's *Hello Children*, wrote
to Enid Blyton to ask whether she would be willing
to be interviewed about the best holiday she could
remember. 'Dear Mr Gamlin,' Blyton wrote the next
day. 'Thank you for your nice letter. It all sounds very
interesting but I ought to warn you of something you
obviously don't know, but which has been well known
in the literary and publishing world for some time – I
and my stories are completely banned by the BBC as
far as children are concerned.'

From Room 432 at Broadcasting House, Gamlin later received a memo addressed to him by Derek
McCulloch, the producer and presenter of Children's
Hour. McCulloch was known to every child growing up
between the mid-1930s and 1950 as 'Uncle Mac' and
was as famous to them as anyone could be. The memo
was marked 'Enid Blyton Stories' and, in red, 'strictly
confidential and urgent'. 'I will be grateful,' McCulloch
wrote, 'if you would first discuss with me should you
be considering the inclusion of material by the above
author. I am most anxious that no conflicts in policy
shall get loose, not only to our embarrassment, but to

yours also.' Gamlin was a company man and he clearly got the point. 'In spite of the desire voiced by some of the children who wrote,' Gamlin replied, 'I have no intention of using any material by the above author, as I think I mentioned to you after I had first approached her without knowing your policy in the matter. Have no fear, there will be No Orchids for Miss B. at any time.' The BBC brass didn't like Blyton's work – 'there is rather a lot of the Pinky-winky-Doodle-doodle Dum-dum type of name' – and Gamlin, glad to have a job, didn't hesitate to overrule what children wanted in order to please Room 432.

Lionel Gamlin, born in Birkenhead in 1903, was a Cambridge graduate who came to broadcasting via acting, a profession he turned to in the mid-1930s after he got tired of being a schoolmaster. He once said he had liked teaching because it kept him young, but acting let him be other people, and in the 1940s he thrived, voicing the RAF documentary *Squadron 992* and appearing as the compere in the variety show *Rainbow Round the Corner*. Along with the BBC's senior announcer, Leslie Mitchell, he became a voice of authority, the tone of war and peace, the man whom people heard in the cinema on the newsreels produced by British Movietone. Gamlin was a star. Terence Gallacher, who worked for Movietone at the time, remembers him visiting the offices at 22 Soho Square once a week. Gamlin was a first-class commentator who rarely made a mistake. 'In those days, before the introduction of magnetic tape,' Gallacher wrote, 'a mistake was quite expensive. The voice was recorded onto 35mm film as an optical soundtrack. If the commentator made a mistake, all the film used up to that point for the sound on a given story had to be junked.'

Gamlin had done well at the BBC making life easier for people who had power. He had a gentle, pleasant manner on air, eventually presenting *In Town Tonight* and *Top of the Form*, and becoming a stalwart of light entertainment broadcasting in the 1950s. He once introduced a talk by George Bernard Shaw. 'Young man,' Shaw said, pointing to the microphone, 'this is a devilish contraption. You can't deceive it – so don't try.' Gamlin later said he remembered all his life the genial advice Shaw had given him. He didn't want to deceive anyone, yet sometimes deception is a way of seeming brave in your own eyes as you go about getting your way.

It was a time of Player's cigarettes and gin after hours at the pubs on Great Portland Street. Broadcasting House was a maze of stairwells, long corridors and unknown powers, a world within worlds that couldn't quite decide whether it was a branch of the civil service or a theatrical den. Many of the men who worked there were getting their own way in the national interest, and the best (or worst) of them combined the secrecy of Whitehall with the languor of Fitzrovia. It was Patrick Hamilton in conversation with George Smiley down a blind alley off Rathbone Place, with froth sliding down the insides of pint tumblers and lipsticked fags in every ashtray. Men such as Gamlin practically lived in Langham Place: their outer bounds were Soho, Bloomsbury, Marylebone, and everything else was the World Service.

In the issue of *Lilliput* magazine for May 1943 Gamlin wrote an essay called 'Why I Hate Boys', which is signed 'A School-Master'. It was a developing theme, boys, children, whatever, and in 1946 Methuen published a book written by Gamlin and Anthony Gilbert called *Don't Be Afreud! A Short Guide to Youth Control (The Book of the Weak)*. The book is just about as funny as it wants to be, with author photographs ('aged 7 and 8 approx') and a caption: 'The authors on their way to the Psychoanalyst'. Gamlin, in common with later youthquakers such as Jimmy Savile, never liked children, never had any, never wanted any, and on the whole couldn't bear them, except on occasion to fuck. And, again like Savile, Gamlin managed all this quite brilliantly, hiding in plain sight as a youth presenter full of good sport but who didn't really care for youth and all its pieties. This was in the days before 'victims' – days that our present media and their audiences find unimaginable – but it gives context and background to the idea of an eccentric presenter as a teasing anti-hero within the Corporation. Auntie was essentially being joshed by a child abuser posing as a child abuser. 'Before we examine the second stage of the malignant disease of Youth with a capital

Y (sometimes conveniently glossed over by the mystic term "adolescence"),' Gamlin wrote in his book, 'it should be remembered that all Youth, like ancient Gaul, is divided into three parts: The Imponderable – The Improbable – The Impossible. No successful treatment is possible if this fundamental division is ignored, for although the three parts combine to make the unwholesome whole, they remain distinct (if revolting) entities, and treatment must vary accordingly.' In Savile's day, a decade on from Gamlin's prime, such avuncular kidding could gain you your own TV show plus charity-god status, an almost nationalised belief in your goodness and zaniness and readiness to help.

But Gamlin lived his double life in the country that existed before Cliff Richard. On the back of his broadcasting fame, and his other interests, he became a spokesman on the tribulations of the Ovalteens. At the Albert Hall in 1949, he followed the Duke of Edinburgh and Clement Attlee in speaking at the *Daily Mail* Youth Forum – an audience of six thousand young people from around the world. He described himself as 'a middle-aged old fogey' (he was 46). 'If Britain's contribution to [a] better world is both important and invaluable,' he said, 'especially in the field, as the prime minister just reminded us, of human relationships, Europe's contribution is no less so. It is fitting, I think, that those young men and women on whom the brunt of the task will fall in a very few years from now, should voice their opinions and ideals.'

A BBC producer from the 1950s told me that he remembers Lionel Gamlin as a person with large ears and a face that seemed to be crumpled in the middle. Unlike the tall and elegant Mitchell, his chief rival, the hero of *Hello Children* was short and round, with a face for radio. Indeed, the onset of television pushed a lot of well-known radio announcers onto the back foot, and several struggled to make the move. Some who did, such as Gilbert Harding (another Cambridge graduate and former schoolteacher, later a famously agitated contestant on *What's My Line?*), were known for their melancholy and their loneliness as well as for their charitable work. Terence Gallacher remembers that Gamlin constantly worried that TV would end his career: 'Lionel complained to anyone willing to listen that he was being ostracised by the BBC Television Service.'

Gamlin liked to help young actors and one colleague, now in his eighties, told me that he was always surrounded by them in Broadcasting House. The actor and director Bryan Forbes, who would go on to direct *Whistle Down the Wind* and *The Stepford Wives*, remembered the help he got from Gamlin. Forbes wrote to him at the BBC – at the time Forbes's name was John Theobald Clarke – and Gamlin wrote back, telling Forbes that his letter was so extraordinary he would have to meet him. When they met Gamlin said it would be necessary for him to change his name. 'Another young actor, ahead of me,' Forbes wrote years later in *Notes for a Life*, 'was also named John Clarke. "You want a good-sounding name," Gamlin said, "and one that looks right on the bills. These things are important."'

A friend of Gamlin's remembers going to see him in a flat in All Souls Place in the 1950s, just round the corner from Broadcasting House. A man from Light Entertainment used the flat during the working week and Gamlin often stayed there with young boys. It was clear to the friend that both men were renting the boys, and that the boys were young: 'They were boys with the kind of good looks that would seem very lewd in a woman.' He also remembers going for a coffee with one of the boys from the flat. 'The boy was nice,' he said, 'very young. He thought he might get a job or something of that sort. And it was clear the men were using him for sex. Broadcasting House was well stocked with men interested in sleeping with young boys. It was a milieu back then. And people who sought to be sexual predators knew that. It wasn't spoken about.'

People who worked at the BBC then are reticent about the sexual habits of the time. They speak like survivors – many of the big names are dead, some for more than forty years – and have an understandable wish to resist the hysteria, the prurience, the general shrieking that surrounds discussions of sexual conduct, whether risky and deviant or not. When I spoke to David Attenborough he was amazed to hear that someone he knew might have been named by others as part of the scene surrounding Gamlin at All Souls Place. I don't hesitate to believe him: he clearly knew nothing about it. Others saw much more than he did and can put names to the people involved, but most of them wanted to tell their stories off the record. The BBC isn't the Catholic Church, but it has its own ideals and traditions, which cause people to pause before naming the unwise acts that have been performed on its premises. Perhaps more than any church, the BBC continues to be a powerhouse of virtue, of intelligence and tolerance, but it is now suffering a kind of ecclesiastical terror at its own fallibility. One has to look further into the institution to see another, more obscure tradition, the one that leads to Savile and his liberty-taking. There was always an element of it waiting to be picked up. Many people I spoke to wished to make that clear, but – feeling the Chorus watching from above – they asked for anonymity.

One presenter told me of being 'grabbed' in Broadcasting House by Malcolm Muggeridge, who spent most of his time in the 1960s railing against the permissive society, 'pot and pills'. The Muggeridge grope wasn't welcomed but it didn't seem totally irregular to the person on the receiving end. She could name at least one other person, a politician, who thought it was OK to put his hand up the skirts of young women at the BBC. It wasn't irregular. What was irregular was the idea of talking about it, even now.

There was a bar nearby where many of the people

who worked at Broadcasting House would meet for drinks during and after working hours. Louis Mac-Neice conferenced there and the Light Entertainment people came and went too, en route to other haunts. A schoolboy who was part of a team that had done well on *Top of the Form* told me Gamlin was extremely sweet to him and 'a nice man all round'. The boy did an interview with him for his school magazine. 'Thanks for the honey-sweet publicity,' Gamlin said. They stayed in touch and the young man knew that Gamlin took it very badly in the mid-1950s when he was deemed unsuitable for TV. 'He was spending a lot of time in Brighton,' the man, who is now in his eighties, told me. 'He ended up as a valet; he was a gentleman's gentleman between infrequent acting jobs – and he once told me the beach at Brighton, this would be in the 1950s, was covered with copies of Angus Wilson's *Hemlock and After*.'

Wilson's novel, pretty much forgotten now, tells the story of a writer called Bernard Sands who is married but homosexual and ends up living next door to a woman, Mrs Curry, who procures children for paedophiles. The book was deemed shocking on publication and would perhaps be thought even more so today, given the way the subject grows and grows to become our chosen national nightmare. Whatever else it has been in the past, paedophilia was always an institutional disorder, in the sense that it has thrived in covert worlds with powerful elites. Boarding schools and hospitals, yes, churches certainly, but also in our premier entertainment labyrinths.

It is becoming clear that Gamlin and his friend at the flat in All Souls Place were not alone in what they were doing. There was at least a third person: Derek McCulloch, 'Uncle Mac', the man in charge of *Children's Hour*, and the voice of Larry the Lamb in *Toytown*. A veteran of the Somme who lost an eye there, McCulloch lost his left leg in a motor accident in the 1930s. He was famous at the BBC for nearly forty years and can still be heard in the archives introducing young Princess Elizabeth as she delivers her wartime address to the children of Britain. 'Goodnight children, everywhere' was Uncle Mac's catchprase.

Though Gamlin's activities were under wraps until now, there have long been rumours about McCulloch. He was given the OBE in 1964 and died in 1967, the same year as Gamlin. Of the three men named to me as I talked to people about the BBC in those days, Uncle Mac is the one who stirs the strongest emotions. In his book *Strange Places, Questionable People*, published in 1998, John Simpson, the BBC's world affairs editor, writes about his early days there. In 1967, he was given the task of preparing the obituary of a famous children's presenter. He calls him 'Uncle Dick'. In 1998, and still today, Simpson felt he shouldn't name McCulloch directly: but it is now clear that Uncle Dick is Uncle Mac. In preparing the obituary, Simpson rang 'Auntie Gladys', who had worked with him, to get a few quotes. 'Week after week,' Auntie Gladys told him, 'children from all over the country would win competitions to visit the BBC and meet Uncle Dick. He would welcome them, show them round, give them lunch, then take them to the gents and interfere with them. If their parents complained, she said, the director-general's office would write and say the nation wouldn't understand such an accusation against a much loved figure.' Auntie Gladys was Kathleen Garscadden, who worked for *Children's Hour* for a number of years and died in 1991. Again, many of the people who worked for her, the actors and singers, are not alive, but some were available to be spoken to. Protégés of hers such as Stanley Baxter never heard her accuse McCulloch. One of her 'young artists' said: 'She would have been at pains to shelter us from any hint of such a thing.' When Simpson reported her remarks to his boss, the man rounded on him and told him he was an 'ignorant, destructive young idiot'. The boss then rewrote Simpson's copy; McCulloch, the obituary now said, 'had a wonderful way with children'. The Corporation turned a blind eye to what was being said about McCulloch just as it later would with Savile and some of the others. Yet people knew. The *Times* obituary of McCulloch was written by the poet Geoffrey Dearmer. 'Children of all ages were always comfortable in his unseen company,' Dearmer wrote. 'There was something of Larry the Lamb in him, and Larry could get away with murder.'

One of the qualities that made the journey from radio to television was 'personality'. Suddenly, you had these human beings who were ultra-everything: they were funnier and quicker and smarter than you – and, once on television, they were prettier, too. At the BBC these people became like gods. Even the weird ones. Even the ones whom everybody could tell were deranged. They had personality and that was the gold standard. Soon enough the notion of 'men being men' was extended, institutionally, into that's just 'Frankie being Frankie' or 'Jimmy being Jimmy'. We never asked whether a certain derangement was a crucial part of their talent.

And so you open Pandora's box to find the seedy ingredients of British populism. It's not just names, or performers and acts, it's an ethos. Why is British light entertainment so often based on the sexualisation of people too young to cope? And why is it that we have a press so keen to feed off it? Is it to cover the fact, via some kind of willed outrage, that the culture itself is largely paedophile in its commercial and entertain-ment excitements? Milly Dowler's phone was hacked by journalists cynically feeding the ravenous appetites of three million people who love that stuff, and that's just the ones who actually bought the *News of the World*. When Leveson's findings are duly buried, will we realise that it was the nation's populist appetites that were on trial all along?

We're not allowed to say it. Because we love our

tots. Or, should I say: WE LOVE OUR TOTS? We know we do because the *Mirror* tells us we do, but would you please get out of the way because you're blocking my view of another fourteen-year-old crying her eyes out on *The X-Factor* as a bunch of adults shatter her dreams. Savile went to work in light entertainment and thrived there: of course he did, because those places were custom-built for men who wanted to dandle dreaming kids on their knees. If you grew up during 'the golden era of British television', the 1970s, when light entertainment was tapping deep into the national unconscious, particularly the more perverted parts, you got used to grown-up men like Rod Hull clowning around on stage with a girl like Lena Zavaroni. You got used to Hughie Green holding the little girl's hand and asking her if she wanted an ice-cream. Far from wanting an ice-cream, the little girl was starving herself to death while helpfully glazing over for the camera and throwing out her hands and singing 'Mama, He's Making Eyes at Me'. She was thirteen.

There's something creepy about British light entertainment and there always has been. Joe Orton meets the Marquis de Sade at the end of the pier, with a few Union Jacks fluttering in the stink and a mother-in-law tied in bunting to a ducking-stool. Those of us who grew up on it liked its oddness without quite understanding how creepy it was. I mean, Benny Hill? And then we wake up one day, in 2012, and wonder why so many of them turned out to be deviants and weirdos.

Our papers explode in outrage and we put on our *Crucible* expressions before setting off to the graveyard to take down the celebrity graves and break them up for landfill. Of course. Graffiti the plaques and take down the statues, because the joy of execration must match the original sin, when we made heroes out of these damaged and damaging 'entertainers'. We suddenly wish them to have been normal, when all we ever ask of our celebrities is that they be much more fucked up than we are. And what do we do now? Do we burn the commemorative programmes, scratch their names from the national memory?

The public made Jimmy Savile. It loved him. It knighted him. The Prince of Wales accorded him special rights and the authorities at Broadmoor gave him his own set of keys. A whole entertainment structure was built to house him and make him feel secure. That's no one's fault: entertainment, like literature, thrives on weirdos, and Savile entered a culture made not only to tolerate his oddness but to find it refreshing. We can't say so. We can't know how to admit it because we don't know who we are. 'This is the worst crisis I can remember in my nearly fifty years at the BBC,' John Simpson said on *Panorama*. 'It's off the scale of everybody's belief system,' said the DJ Paul Gambaccini.

But it *is* our belief system. And now it is part of the same system to blame Savile. He's dead, anyway. Let's blame him for all the things he obviously was, and blame him for a host of other things we don't understand, such as how we love freaks and how we select and protect people who are 'eccentric' in order to feed our need for disorder. We'll blame him for that too and say we never knew there would be any victims, when, in fact, we depend on there being victims. Savile just wouldn't have been worth so much to us without his capacity to hurt. He was loved for being so rich and so generous and for loving his mother, the Duchess. And no one said, not out loud: 'What's wrong with that man? Why is he going on like that? What is he up to?' He was an entertainer and that's thought to be special. A more honest society brings its victims to the Colosseum and cheers. We agreed to find it OK when our most famous comedians were clearly not OK. When Benny Hill's mother died, in 1976, he kept her house in Southampton as a shrine, just as Savile kept his mother's clothes, and it might have been weird but it was also the kind of celebrity eccentricity we had come to expect.

Day by day over the past month details have emerged about the shelving of the *Newsnight* investigation into Savile. Girls from Duncroft children's home had given evidence: some of them were fourteen when Savile began coercing them into giving him blowjobs. They felt it would be 'an honour' to be in the company of someone so famous. He promised them visits to the BBC studios and one of them says she saw Gary Glitter having sex with another girl who was also from Duncroft in a BBC dressing-room. 'Did Duncroft, a

well-equipped approved school for "intelligent emo-
tionally disturbed girls" in leafy Surrey, really require
the patronage of "Uncle" Jimmy Savile?' Dan Davies
asks in his unpublished book about Savile:

Many of the 25 or so girls in its care at any one time came from
comfortable backgrounds and included the daughters of am-
bassadors and BBC producers. As a Home Office-approved
school, funding came from Social Services. Regular guests
at their parties included the actor James Robertson Justice,
who was one of Britain's leading film stars in the 1940s and
1950s and reportedly a close friend of the Duke of Edinburgh.
Princesses Marina and Alexandra are said to have attended.
Among the former Duncroft girls to have come forward, one
has said she was put in the isolation unit for 'two or three days'
after loudly protesting when Savile groped her in a caravan on
the school grounds. 'For years we tried to report him,' another confided to me. 'We even had a mass breakout to Staines
police station.'

The *Newsnight* programme was well sourced and
strong, but it clashed – in the old-fashioned, schedul-
ing sense – with two tributes to Savile the BBC had
planned. The investigations will continue, but the bigger story is missing from all the discussions around
Savile, the bigger story being the milieu that existed
not only at the BBC but in the light entertainment
firmament.

Gamlin's BBC friend from All Souls Place,
where the underage boys used to come and visit, was

responsible for some of the landmark comedy shows at the BBC. He was also part of the team that came up with the idea of *Top of the Pops* and launched it on New Year's Day 1964 with a presenter called Jimmy Savile. The birth of rock'n'roll had a complicated relationship with the coming of the permissive society. Asa Briggs, in his history of the BBC, documents the struggle in which sexual freedoms and sexual norms were bent out of shape: for every permissive moment there was a shadow of the not-permitted. And so, not long before we had Orton and *Entertaining Mr Sloane*, we had Mr Tom Sloan of BBC Light Entertainment threatening to drop Marty Wilde from the fledgling pop show *Six-Five Special* on account of his 'Presley-type belly-swinging'.

Fame was a new kind of licence. And presenters at the BBC were suddenly even more famous than Gamlin had been. Sexual intercourse began, if Larkin's your man, in 1963 – a year before *Top of the Pops* – and off the back of the *Lady Chatterley* trial and the Beatles' first LP. But the intermediaries, too, were now part of the strange dance of the permissive with the banned. And it became part of their public profile to thrive at the centre of a doubt about acceptability. That might be one way of thinking about Jimmy Savile getting the keys to Broadmoor. After 1964, and perhaps not before it, familiarity bought you unlimited trust from the public. Suddenly, the greatest virtue of them all was fame – that was fame before celebrity, which brought other favours but also drawbacks. Savile was so famous it blotted out any of the other obvious things about him, and that is a deal we're still living with. 'These men, people like Jimmy Savile, were treated like rock stars,' Joan Bakewell said when I asked her about him. 'And sexually many of those men lived in a self-contained culture.' Bakewell was working as a studio manager in those days and she saw how available and how willing many of the young people were. 'People were at the top of their form and many were jubilantly having affairs,' she says. 'The homosexual element was murkier. You just didn't hear about it. We'd drink in the George, round the corner from Broadcasting House. Sensuality lay in drink – those men with red faces. People like MacLaren-Ross would be sponging for money and it all seemed excessive but fine.'

'And Jimmy Savile?'

'Later, yes. Repellent, you know. He once tried to get me to go to his hotel room. But many of the young girls who did go I'm afraid went willingly.'

Bakewell says it's odd to see how the ethos now looks so horrible and so bent. 'You can't re-create the mood of an era,' she said. 'You just can't get into the culture of what it was like, transfer our sensibilities backwards from today. It would be like asking Victorian factory owners to explain why they sent children up chimneys. It's the same with the BBC that I first entered. It had habits and values that we just can't understand from the point of view of where we are now.

What we now find unacceptable was just accepted back then by many people.'

Gilbert Harding, a refugee from the culture of the Light Programme – a man who made his way into TV memory by weeping on John Freeman's television interview show *Face to Face* – was a stalwart of the milieu inhabited by Gamlin and company. A man can't help whom he fancies, but Harding seems to have differed from the other BBC paedophiles only inasmuch as he kept it mainly to himself. He had spent his childhood in a Wolverhampton orphanage and maintained he wanted to die long before he actually did, stepping out of Broadcasting House after a radio recording on 16 November 1960 to collapse on the pavement. A writer who knew Harding told me he was another of those, like Gamlin, who liked to enter into correspondence with schoolboys. On one occasion the writer was taken from school to visit Harding for tea (the headmaster was dazzled), whereupon Harding insisted the boy take a bath and scrub himself with soap while the gameshow veteran sat watching him. 'Harding was a rather disturbed individual,' the BBC presenter Nicholas Parsons told me. 'Nowadays a man with troubles of that sort would be in therapy.'

Child abuse is now a national obsession, but in 1963 it scarcely came up as a subject of public concern. That doesn't mean it was fine back then and we were all better off, but it allows one to see how much the public understanding of what isn't all right, or more or less all right, has changed. There have always been genuine causes for concern, but overall, nowadays there is an unmistakeable lack of proportion in the way we talk about the threat posed to children by adults. (It's hard not to imagine that the situation has to do with a general estrangement from the notion of a reliable community.) The 1960s, on the other hand, seem like a sexual kaleidoscope made of unusual colours, out of focus, out of order, but not 'out'. There is always a dark lining to permission – asking for it, granting it – and 1963 was a moment of blurring more than a moment of clarity. Women might have worn shorter skirts and gone on the pill but society still didn't – and still doesn't – sexually know itself as well as it might.

Light entertainment was a big, double-entendre-filled department, of interest to brilliant deviants. By 'deviants' I mean anybody who wasn't in a monogamous heterosexual marriage that produced children. And many in that position too were deviant in 1963, when it was unclear where sexual power began and ended. It wasn't merely the time of Christine Keeler and Mandy Rice-Davies, the time of the Cliveden set, *Up the Junction* and *Carry on Camping*. It was also the time of the Polari-speaking world of the Colony Room and the Gargoyle Club, filled with the kind of people sent up by Julian and Sandy in the BBC's *Round the Horne*. I once asked John Peel, the late Radio 1 DJ, about the tendency in his youth for people (including him) not to be fussed about how young their girlfriends were. (Peel was briefly married to someone in America who was fifteen and he made the point that one just couldn't tell, and one wasn't inclined to ask, how old people were.) But Peel went on to describe the kind of abuse that was common at boarding school, with nobody really complaining. He suffered some of that himself and didn't go on about it, but he made the point that the famous freedoms of the period were really more like confusions. The 1960s weren't tolerant, as they are said to have been, they were mixed up: people say it felt as though sexual freedom was on the increase but many proclivities couldn't and shouldn't be free and the era had a very odd way of dealing with them. There was the funny world of *Julian and Sandy*, but, behind it, there was also the world of Joe Orton and Kenneth Halliwell having regular sex with fourteen-year-old boys. Peggy Ramsay encouraged Orton to keep a journal 'à la Gide' about their time in Morocco. The diaries are a long whirling trip of hashish and sex, full of what John Lahr, who edited Orton's diaries, called 'the cockeyed liberty of the time'. A Tangier acquaintance, a 45-year-old Englishman called Nigel, told Orton he liked young boys.

'How young?'

'Oh very young.'

'But how young? Twelve?'

'Oh no, about fourteen.'

'Oh, perfectly natural.'

The cockeyed-ness is evident when you look at the diaries of Orton's friend Kenneth Williams, who was happy to come to Morocco but whose diaries blench at the mere thought of liberated sex:

Thursday, 26 September 1963: The Denning Report on the Profumo-Ward case is out. Apparently it says that well-known actors were at these filthy parties. It is a disgrace that such people should bring our profession into disrepute in this vile way. Thank the powers that my own private fantasies have been left to wrestle with my own conscience and not in physical acts with others.

Orton wrote letters to Williams using the name Uncle Whuppity, one of them offering advice to children about how to avoid the clap.

I asked Nicholas Parsons about Kenneth Williams. 'He was inhibited and tortured,' Parsons said, 'and was trying to embrace the new freedom but didn't know how to do it properly. Some people can't escape from the attitudes and conditions laid upon them by their parents and Kenneth had a very difficult childhood.'

'And what about Orton and company?' I asked.

'They probably allowed Kenneth to express that other side of his nature,' Parsons said. 'I mean, that's the thing about those freedoms in the 1960s: it was wonderful to have it, but it also included the freedom to reject it. We weren't all dropping our inhibitions and dropping our trousers. And there were still some very conservative elements. I remember I was working at the Savoy, it was before *Lady Chatterley*, and the Wolfenden Report had just come out. I made some joke saying "Homo Adds Brightness" – there was an advertisement for Omo washing powder along those lines – and the management was horrified.'

'If you're going to be an entertainer you have to accept that you're an odd human being,' he said in response to one of my questions. 'You have to be a little bit mad to succeed in that world.'

'Odd, yes. Mad even,' I said, 'but deviant?'

'No,' he said. 'Definitely not. Not everyone at the BBC, or anywhere else for that matter, will be a shining example of rectitude. The BBC is a fantastic place, though, and these weird exceptions can't tarnish it. Savile was immoral and disgusting but not typical, not to me.'

People can like children in the wrong way. And there no doubt is a wrong way. So when you see Gilbert Harding crying about his impossible self, you may feel very sorry. You may feel, as many people who liked Lionel Gamlin felt, that these were talented people whose paedophilia constituted a difficulty for them as well as for others. This was the milieu – so far unmentioned in all the hoohah – that Jimmy Savile entered when he left Radio Luxembourg. But nobody will feel sorry for him because he was made to the public's specifications and to the specifications of the tabloid press, which has the skill to carry both the public's worst fantasies and its deepest shame into print. For forty years people believed Savile was the hero of Stoke Mandeville Hospital and for forty years the red-top papers promoted his image as the nation's zaniest and most lovable donor. He may have abused two hundred children during that time.

I met Dan Davies, Savile's biographer, when he was deputy editor of *Esquire* and was writing his book. He always said the story was seedy and strange and that when the book was published he would call it 'Apocalypse Now Then'. He met up with Savile in transport cafés or at home in Scarborough, had supper with him at the Athenaeum, followed him onto the QE2. 'It's a dark story,' Davies said years ago. 'But it's our childhood, you know.' Savile was not an intelligent person, he was also defensive, exploitative and furious. At some level, he got away with everything because the nation wanted him to, taking to him like a long-running alibi. Bosses and colleagues who knew what he was doing say he was just being Jimmy. And he was just Jimmy to the public as well. It is the kind of concession a sentimental society makes to its worst deviants. Live and let live: he's just being Jimmy. And if there were worries then the worries got buried, just as the BBC buried that *Newsnight* story.

Victim Support lawyers are now talking about an endemic culture of sexual misconduct at the BBC. ('What? A paedophile ring at the BBC?' asked the consternated reporter Shelley Jofre on *Panorama*.) But when the lawyers look for evidence they should look to the culture itself to find proper answers. Until now, no one thought to examine *Children's Hour* and the world around it, much less the payola scandal involving radio DJs in the first flush of Savile's fame. Janie Jones, a singer, appeared at Bow Street Magistrates' Court in 1973 on 26 charges, which included controlling prostitutes and offering them as bribes 'to BBC men as inducement to play records'. The men in the case were often referred to as Mr Z or Mr Y, or 'unnamed broadcasters'. The court heard how Mr Y, 'a television producer', might have made a fourteen-year-old girl pregnant and could therefore be blackmailed. Mr X later answered questions about a cheque for £100 he gave to one of the girls but said he didn't know she was a prostitute. 'I thought she was much too young to be involved in anything like that,' he said in court. Others remanded on bail included Jack Dabbs, a former producer of the radio programme *Worldwide Family Favourites*, Len Tucker, a theatrical agent, and several record promoters. At the time of the trial arrest warrants were out for members of the New World pop group who had won TV's *Opportunity Knocks* ten times. The big trial that followed is now forgotten. According to *The Time*s, 'a shop assistant, aged eighteen, referred to as Miss G, said at the Central Criminal Court yesterday that Miss Jones said she could get work in modelling and television commercials, but she must play her cards right.'

'Playing her cards' meant going to bed with producers and showbusiness people.

'I was very interested in the work, but not in going to bed with producers,' she said . . . Miss G agreed that Miss Jones had taken her a couple of times to the *Top of the Pops* show at Shepherd's Bush . . . 'All I saw were a bunch of little kids jumping up and down.'

Peter Dow, QC, for Miss Jones, asked: 'Some of them got a chance that way?'

'Having lived with Janie,' Miss G replied, 'I know the scene inside out and it sickens me when I think about it.'

'Radio 1 was well known to be a law unto itself,' a BBC broadcaster from the 1960s told me. And Jimmy Savile would be safe there for nearly fifty years. 'The BBC is a big family,' Savile said to Louis Theroux. 'Turn over any family stone and you will find all sorts of peculiar goings on. Our family is no worse than any-body else's.' Savile not only entered a culture of sexual anxiety: he *was* a culture of sexual anxiety. The fact was spotted by an anxious boss figure from that time, Tom Sloan, who became head of Light Entertainment in 1961. He was the man who was worried by Marty Wilde's swinging pelvis, but he was also worried about Savile, and an engine of worries, according to some. In 1959, the new pop show *Juke Box Jury* was produced by Johnnie Stewart. 'I wanted to use Jim [Savile] as a bit of variety to give David Jacobs a little break,' Stew-art explains in *The Story of 'Top of the Pops'*. 'My boss at the time, the late Tom Sloan, said: "I don't want that man on the television." I said: "Sorry baby, but that man is box office. In his own sweet way – boy is he box office." It is true to say that with his two-tone non-regulation hair, a somewhat bizarre taste in clothes and his rather buoyant personality, Jimmy Savile was not the typical "righter than right" BBC presenter.'

It would take another 53 years for Savile to be unmasked. And the BBC employed him for nearly all of that time and the nation loved him. If the Savile story – and the stories that constitute a hinterland at the BBC – turn out to involve a great conspiracy, it will be a conspiracy that the whole country had a part in. There will always be a certain amount of embarrassment about Savile, not because we didn't know but because we did. I contacted Dan Davies to see how things were going with the sale of his book. Turns out every major publisher had turned it down. 'It remains,' Dan said, 'the biography everyone wants to read but no publisher has the balls to publish. Just 140,000 words of interviews over six years, days and nights spent talking to him at his various homes, thousands of miles of ocean crossed in his company, scores of friends; associates hunted down and grilled. The millstone gets heavier and heavier. Let me know if you need anything – quotes, background, detail, a stetson hat given to him by Elvis Presley in 1962.' I emailed him back immediately, telling him to hold the stetson. I then asked whether he knew anything about Lionel Gamlin and the old guard at Broadcasting House. 'He was an old actor, wasn't he?' Davies replied. 'Part of a paedo ring at the BBC, I presume.'

Later that evening I went to look at All Souls Place. The BBC has recently expanded into it and the houses have gone, replaced by a shiny new extension. Outside, reporters wrapped in scarves delivered pieces to camera about the current crisis. I wonder if any of them know about the old flats.

Sameer Rahim

– The Shadow of the Scroll –
Reconstructing Islam's Origins

I n the year 777, the Caliph al-Mahdi performed a pilgrimage in the sacred city of Medina. He visited the mosque where the Prophet Muhammad had been buried 145 years earlier. Mahdi was pleased to see still standing the wooden pulpit from which the Prophet had delivered the Friday sermon. But he was dismayed to discover that an earlier caliph had transformed the pulpit to make it look more grandly magnificent. He ordered his carpenters to remove the additions and re-store the pulpit to its original simplicity. But when they examined the structure more closely they discovered that the earlier caliph's iron nails had been driven so deep that pulling them out would risk destroying the entire edifice. Mahdi left the pulpit untouched.

Modern Muslim attitudes towards the birth of Is-lam are haunted by a similar caution. While most agree that the Prophet's life story has over 1,400 years been overlaid with fictional accretions, Muslims have been notably reluctant to strip them away. There remains a persistent fear that, as with the Prophet's pulpit, once the supports are removed the original story will come crashing down. Over the last 40 years, however, West-ern academics, inspired by the higher criticism first

112

applied to Christianity in the nineteenth century, have posed troubling questions regarding the traditional Islamic story. How reliable are our accounts of the Prophet? Was the Qu'ran revealed on one miraculous night or collected long after his death? Did Muhammad grow up in Mecca and then move to Medina? Did he even exist? To a Muslim it might seem absurd or even blasphemous to ask such questions: there is already a settled story about Islam's origins with reams of supporting evidence. Yet any Muslim studying Islamic history at a Western university will find scepticism embedded in the curriculum. More importantly a historical reappraisal of Islam offers the vital chance of religious renewal. During a time when Muslims across the world are struggling to accommodate their faith with modernity – including the present writer – much can be gained from taking another look at what exactly the Prophet did and said during the early seventh century, and what later commentators projected on him during the first flowering of Islamic scholarship.

THE DEBATE

According to the traditional narrative, Muhammad was born in 570 in a pagan town called Mecca in northeast Arabia. Orphaned at an early age, he worked the caravan routes to Syria and Yemen, where he came into contact with Christians and Jews. While on these trips he met a widow called Khadija, whom he married. As time passed he became disillusioned with his world and began meditating in a mountain cave outside Mecca. When he was forty years old something extraordinary happened during one of his spiritual retreats. A voice rang out:

Recite, in the name of your Lord! He who created man from an embryo. Recite! Your Lord is most bountiful. He taught with the pen. He taught man what he knew not.

This was the first of many divine revelations he received until his death twenty-two years later, which were collected in a book called the Qu'ran – or 'the Recitation'. Muhammad began preaching his belief in a single God, and declared himself a prophet in the line of Moses and Jesus. His wife Khadija converted along with family members and a few outside the Meccan elite – mostly slaves and immigrants. But his early ministry was a popular failure.

The turning point came in 622, when the leaders of an oasis 200 miles north of Mecca invited Muhammad to become their leader. His migration to Medina, known as the *Hijra*, marked the start of the Muslim calendar. In the new city, Muhammad's mission changed from warning of God's impending judgment to building a community. His followers needed guidance on day-to-day life and his revelations accordingly began to include more legal rulings. The Prophet negotiated a concord with nearby Jewish tribes known as

the 'Constitution of Medina'. He sent raiding parties
to attack the Meccans and in 630 the Prophet's home-
town surrendered. He removed the pagan images
hanging inside the sacred shrine – a stone cube called
the Ka'aba – and performed the pilgrimage. Then he
returned to Medina where he died in 632.

This story, familiar to all Muslims, has been re-told
by western historians since Islam began to be studied
seriously by Edward Gibbon. Twentieth-century biographers of Muhammad such as Montgomery Watt and
Karen Armstrong might be sceptical of the miraculous
tales told about the Prophet – splitting the moon with
his finger, for example – but they never seriously doubt
the traditional framework. Since the September 11 attacks against America, anti-Islamic polemics familiar
from medieval times have been resurgent. Debates
over how the Prophet treated his wives, his dealings
with Jews and the heavenly reward for martyrs are
invoked to explain modern terrorist atrocities. In response Muslims quote stories about the Prophet's gen-
erosity and tolerance. Their interpretations are wildly
different but both sides use the same diverse source
material. Even that most controversial work, Salman
Rushdie's novel *The Satanic Verses* (1988), is rooted in
the Islamic tradition. The novel revolves round an incident in Mecca when a beleaguered Prophet is allowed
by God to admit pagan deities as religious intercessors
– only for the revelation to be rescinded when it turns
out he has been misguided by the devil's whispers. The

story, which can be found in the Prophet's earliest biography, is far from being the fantastical invention of a twentieth-century author. Rushdie has written with confidence about the reliability of Islamic history: 'The degree of authority one can give to the evangelists about the life of Christ is relatively small. Whereas for the life of Muhammad, we know everything more or less. We know where he lived, what his economic situation was, who he fell in love with. We know a great deal about the political circumstances and the socio-economic circumstances of the time.' But is Rushdie's faith warranted? Some historians are less sanguine.

Last autumn Channel Four broadcast a documentary entitled *Islam: The Untold Story*. Presented by Tom Holland and based on his book *In the Shadow of the Sword*, the programme challenged long-held assumptions about the Prophet's life. Holland, primarily a historian of the ancient world and a relative newcomer to the field, told us that he had assumed from reading Muhammad's English biographers that there existed a wealth of primary documentation – eyewitness reports, letters and inscriptions – dating from the Prophet's time. But on closer inspection he found almost nothing. The first surviving Life of the Prophet was written 220 years after his death – much longer than the distance between Jesus and the Gospels. Given such a chasm almost anything could have been invented, argued Holland, who went on to make some eye-catching claims. Muhammad, he said, was not born in a pagan town in Arabia called Mecca but somewhere closer to Jerusalem. The numerous Qu'ranic references to Biblical stories indicate he preached in the Christian-Jewish milieu in Syria. He also questioned whether the Arabs who conquered the Middle East after the Prophet's death were really Muslims. Perhaps, he continued, they invented a religion and elevated a holy man to prophetic status in order to justify their conquests. He questioned whether the Qu'ran, that holiest of holies, was formed in the way the tradition describes and suggested that later commentators might have strangled interpretation to explain away discomfiting truths.

Muslim reaction to Holland ranged from astonishment to outrage. If Mecca is not Mecca then Muslims have been praying in the wrong direction for 1,400 years; if the Prophet was an Arab invention the spiritual advice and moral guidance embodied in the stories Muslims tell about him turn to dust. Channel Four received 1,200 complaints and Holland was sent abusive messages on Twitter – some disturbingly violent. Muslim intellectuals were equally contemptuous. Reviewing *In the Shadow of the Sword* earlier that year, Zia Sardar accused Holland of being 'besotted by his guru, the Danish Orientalist Patricia Crone' – on whose work Holland draws extensively and whom he interviewed for the TV documentary – and compared the Princeton professor's reputation in Islamic circles to David Irving's in Holocaust studies. From a different perspective, Glen Bowersock, an academic expert on Roman Arabia, labelled Holland's work 'irresponsible', claiming his book was written in a 'swashbuckling style that aims more to unsettle his readers than to instruct them'. Both Sardar and Bowersock implied that Holland was exploiting unease about Muslim immigration to Europe.

The accusation of anti-Islamic prejudice is unwarranted. The front cover of Holland's book barely highlights the controversial material within and he made efforts to constructively engage with Muslims. Simply dismissing his work is wrong-headed. His intervention was the opening salvo in a popular discussion about Islam's origins that will have a profound effect on the religion – comparable to what happened to Christianity when the quest began for the historical Jesus. The mosques, madrasas and seminaries of the Muslim world rarely address such arguments. Religious universities from Cairo to Qom follow the intellectual tradition developed by Muslim scholars in the eighth and ninth centuries – and while their achievements cannot be dismissed easily, their methodology is open to question. Those Muslims wishing to challenge the sceptics must take their arguments seriously. This means learning from their insights and using non-Muslim historical sources and archaeology to check the tradition. Through this process, Muslims can critically re-examine the medieval consensus over what the Prophet said and how the Qu'ran was interpreted; rather than feel threatened, the faithful should embrace the chance to reconstruct Islam from its origins.

THE QU'RAN

The patriarch of the revisionists was an enigmatic SOAS scholar named John Wansbrough. His two books, *Qu'ranic Studies* (1977) and *The Sectarian Milieu* (1978), sought to wholly dismantle the received version of Islam's formation. Applying a special type of literary analysis influenced by deconstruction, Wansbrough came to startling and novel conclusions about the origins of Muslim scripture. Until then everyone had agreed that the Qu'ran – whether divinely inspired or not – was a reasonably accurate reflection of Muhammad's utterances between 610 and 632. Wansbrough dismantled that assumption. In an elliptical prose style that echoed the allusive style of Qu'ranic Arabic, Wansbrough argued that the holy book was not collected within twenty years of the Prophet's death – as tradition has it – but concocted over 200 years using Christian and Jewish oral stories. A close examination of its literary topoi and linguistic repetitions, said Wansbrough, revealed that the Qu'ran was a mish-mash of non-Arabian material.

Wansbrough also broke the intimate link between the Qu'ran and the Prophet's life. Many verses are supposed to have been revealed in response to a particular occasion and Muslim commentators have worked hard to connect them with when and where they appeared. Take the chapter entitled 'The Spoils of War'. The story goes that following the Battle of Badr in 624 – a successful skirmish between the Prophet and his Meccan enemies – the believers fell out over the booty. After divine consultation, Muhammad solved the dispute with the following verse: 'The spoils of war belong to God and His Messenger. So fear God, settle your disputes, and obey God and His Messenger, if you are true believers.' The money was given to the Prophet for him to distribute.

But if the Qu'ran was not contemporary with the Prophet's life, as Wansbrough argued, then the tight-knit relationship between verse and battle is a later elaboration. Imagine the following scenario: Muslim soldiers in, say, the eighth century are arguing with the caliph over who gets the spoils. There is a story floating around concerning the division of booty after the Battle of Badr. A concerned caliph directs a religious expert to invent a verse sanctioning his right to claim it; this verse is then inserted into a still malleable Qu'ran. In Wansbrough's words, 'the exegesis precedes the revelation' – the story came first and then the verse. This radical switch round calls into serious question both the nature of the Qu'ran and the canonical Islamic story.

Wansbrough's theory has not gone unchallenged. Fred Donner, another scholar interviewed by Holland for his documentary and who could be described as a middle-ground revisionist, took up the debate in *Narratives of Islamic Origins* (1998). Donner argued that if the Qu'ran had been put together over 200 years, one would expect it to be filled with anachronistic predictions about people and events – yet it lacks almost any historical data. Perhaps the commentators who supposedly compiled the text edited out these references to make it seem more authentically antique; but since Wansbrough does not identify exactly who put together the Qu'ran, or when, or where, this claim seems far-fetched.

Donner also picked up on the lexical discontinuity between the Qu'ran and the *hadith* – the stories about the Prophet that Wansbrough believed were written at a similarly later date, and by the same people. Take the word for ship: the Qu'ran uses two different terms, *fulk* (24 times) and *safina* (four times). In the *hadith* only the word *safina* is used and in Qu'ran commentaries the unusual word *fulk* – which Donner speculates derives from the word *efólkion* found in Greek sailors' patois – required glossing. If the Qu'ran and the *hadith* had been written at the same time you would expect them to use the same word. In addition the German Qu'ran specialist Angelika Neurwirth detected a stylistic unity in the Meccan chapters that led her to conclude that they were created by a single voice over a short period – not multiple voices over a long time. Literary analysis is debatable territory. More reliable evidence for the Qu'ran's authenticity emerged forty years ago during the renovation of the Sana'a Grand Mosque in Yemen. Bundled in some abandoned sacks were a number of eighth-century Qu'ranic manuscripts that substantially matched the canonical text. Even Holland acknowledges that 'the bedrock of the Qu'ran appears hewn out of solid granite'.

Yet there are some fascinating alternative readings in the Sana'a manuscripts – especially in the chapter order. According to tradition, in the 640s the third caliph asked the Prophet's scribe Zaid ibn Thabit to compile the Qu'ran from men who had memorised the verses or written them down on camel bones or palm-fronds. Zaid's arrangement was not chronological or thematic; he appears to have simply put the long chapters at the front and the short ones at the back. Not all Muslims were happy with his choices. When the caliph's men went round destroying alternative compilations, one rival companion living in Iraq refused to hand his over. 'I prefer to read according to the recitation of the Prophet whom I love,' declared Ibn Mas'ud from the pulpit; 'I learnt more than seventy chapters from the apostle's own lips, while Zaid ibn Thabit was a youth.' Though Ibn Mas'ud's codex has been lost the list of his alternative chapter order survives. In his version the chapter entitled 'The Poets' (26 in the current codex) led straight on to 'Arrayed in Ranks' (37). In one Yemen Qu'ran fragment a page shows 'The Poets' followed by 'Arrayed in Ranks'.

Muslims sometimes claim that the Qu'ran was

revealed in a single night during Ramadan, and that each word we have is exactly as the Prophet spoke it. History, though, has undeniably shaped our text. The Qu'ran evolved in stages from its inception in 610 to its probable codification in the 650s. Later verses superseded earlier ones, as the Muslim theologian Fazlur Rahman has pointed out in *Major Themes of the Qu'ran* (1980). The most famous example of this is the stage-by-stage prohibition of alcohol. First of all believers were told to stop going to prayers drunk (4:43); then the Prophet was instructed that regarding wine and gambling, 'There is great sin in both, and some benefit for people: the sin is greater than the benefit' (2:219); finally, drinking was unambiguously described as 'repugnant' (5:90–1). Placing the Qu'ran more firmly within its historical context will help to emancipate its spiritual message from its legal rulings.

'The language of a historical report is also the language of fiction,' wrote Wansbrough channelling Roland Barthes. 'The difference between the two is a psychological assumption shared by writer and reader, and it is from that assumption that the historical report acquires significance, is deemed worthy of preservation and transmission.' After his burst of activity in the late Seventies, Wansbrough never published a proper book (though he did apparently compose fiction in the manner of Malcolm Lowry). It was his disciples who turned their laser scepticism on the canonical Muslim biographies of the Prophet.

THE MAN

Anyone comparing the work of Tom Holland and Zia Sardar might be puzzled by their wildly divergent claims over when the Prophet's biography was written. Holland regards the only securely dateable work to be a book that has survived from the pen of Ibn Hisham, an Iraqi scholar who lived 200 years after the Prophet – more than twice the time between Jesus's life and the Gospels. Sardar, by contrast, claims there is no such black hole between the Prophet and Ibn Hisham: he cites eyewitness accounts by contemporary companions who noted either in memory or in writing the manners and morals of Muhammad. How do we explain the disagreement?

Ibn Hisham was not a historian in the modern sense: he collected and edited existing chronicles. His biography is a recension of an earlier work by the Medinan Ibn Ishaq, which appeared 120 years after the Prophet's death. Ibn Ishaq's Life, which in English runs to 700 pages, has been reconstructed from Ibn Hisham and later historians who made copies from a lost original. Ibn Ishaq obtained his material from people who knew people who knew people who knew the Prophet. Among his sources he describes 'a trustworthy informant', 'a man of good memory' and 'an old man in Mecca some 40 or more years ago'. Sometimes he lists a chain of transmission – I heard from so-and-so who heard it from so-and-so and so forth. These links form the spine of Islamic historical authenticity.

One of Ibn Ishaq's best sources was Urwa ibn al-Zubayr (d.712). Urwa attached himself to his aunt Ayesha, the Prophet's youngest wife and the daughter of the first caliph. Many stories about the Prophet's early struggles can be traced back to his pillow talk with Ayesha. Urwa also sought out others who had known the Prophet. According to Tarif Khalidi, an expert on Islamic historiography, he was 'an interrogator, a man who questioned his informants closely in search of accuracy'. Khalidi discerns a literary unity in his reports that indicates they were written down rather than orally transmitted. Ibn Ishaq personally received Urwa's findings from Urwa's student al-Zuhri (d.742).

One scandalous tale involving Ayesha shows how such stories were passed down. While travelling on a desert journey with the Prophet, Ayesha strayed from camp to answer the call of nature. While she dilly-dallied over a broken necklace her palanquin-bearers left without realising she was absent. (Ayesha pointedly tells us she ate only 'small rations' and weighed little.) Fortunately, a passing Muslim soldier escorted her back to Medina. On her return, though, rumours begin to swirl about what might have happened between the Prophet's young wife and the handsome soldier. Muhammad was unsettled. He asked his son-in-law Ali for advice. 'Women are plentiful,' replied Ali, 'you can easily change one for another.' Yet Ayesha remained defiant. 'Never will I repent towards God of what you mention,' she told her parents, since that would mean 'admitting that which did not happen'. The Prophet asked for divine guidance. When God answered it was good news for Ayesha: 'This is obviously a lie,' the Qu'ran declared, adding that adultery cases now required four witnesses to the sexual act (24:11). So while Islamic law prescribes severe penalties for fornication (100 lashes), the burden of proof makes conviction almost impossible. For this we have forgetful Ayesha to thank.

This incident in particular has the ring of historical truth. Ayesha related it, and it seems the kind of gossip-rich tale people would have loved to repeat. It is also directly referred to in the Qu'ran in the verse that exonerated her. Examining the chain of transmission, though, you could be forgiven for raising an eyebrow. The desert affair occurred in the 620s and Ayesha talked to Urwa before her death in 678; Urwa wrote it down or informed his student Zuhri before his death in 712; Ibn Ishaq noted the story in 750; and, finally, we read his account in the edited version of Ibn Hisham from the 820s. As well as Chinese whispers, any number of other factors might have affected the telling – not least Ayesha's subsequent involvement in the Civil War that followed the Prophet's death, in which she fought against Ali, the same man she claimed told her husband to discard her.

Early Muslims were deeply concerned with the problem of verifying reports about the Prophet. To model your life upon him means knowing whether he said and did the things claimed; it was literally a matter of salvation or damnation. A transmitter was assessed on his personal piety, general trustworthiness and practical factors such as whether his life overlapped with the person he claimed was his informant, and whether they could have feasibly met. Fabrication was clearly an enormous problem: one respected ninth-century collector of *hadith* – short narratives about the Prophet with little historical information, but which were used for legal purposes – claimed to have found 600,000, of which he dismissed 593,000 as false.

Even within the material classified as sound there are contradictions. The Prophet, for example, is reported as saying that you can rebel against a corrupt caliph, and also that it is forbidden to do so. In the 1950s, the German scholar Joseph Schacht – whose work inspired Wansbrough – cast doubt on the narratives traditionally regarded as being iron cast. His starting presumption was that a story was guilty until proven innocent: 'Every legal tradition from the Prophet, until the contrary is proved, must be taken not as an authentic, even if slightly obscured, statement valid for his time or the time of his companions but as fictitious expressions of a legal doctrine formulated at a later date.'

Two of Wansbrough's pupils, Patricia Crone and Michael Cook, pushed Schacht's thesis to its radical conclusion. Since extracting historical truth from the Muslim tradition is so messy, why not make a clean break and step completely outside it? In *Hagarism* (1977), Crone and Cook presented an account of Islam's rise that relied solely on previously under-explored Christian and Jewish sources for the Proph-et's life, mostly written closer to the Prophet's time than Ibn Ishaq's biography. The title *Hagarism* refers to the name that the first Christian witnesses gave to the invading Arabs: Hagarenes or the sons of Hagar. The authors proposed an elaborate theory that said Islam was a Jewish heresy that only became an inde-pendent religion when the Arabs had a powerful em-pire and needed a dramatic back-story. Their tone was as provocative as their conclusions. 'Written by infidels for infidels', in the authors' words, *Hagarism* ended by explaining why Muslim culture was so retarded as compared with the West's. 'Just as the single source of the Islamic tradition accounts for the austerely unitary character of so much of Islamic history,' they wrote, 'so also the plurality of sources of the culture of Europe is a precondition for its complex historical evolution.'

Crone and Cook published a year before Edward Said's *Orientalism*, and their book was criticised for echoing the anti-Muslim polemics from which they quoted. Yet whatever its flaws, *Hagarism* sparked a rev-olution in Islamic studies. Until that point few scholars had ever properly compared Ibn Ishaq with Christian and Jewish sources. Muslims wondered what non-believers could tell them that was not already in their voluminous histories; while Western Arabists were in disciplinary purdah, unwilling to analyse Greek and Syriac chronicles traditionally the domain of Near East experts. The result was that all the modern Western biographies of Muhammad were, in Crone's words, 'Muslim chronicles in modern languages and graced with modern titles.' Since *Hagarism*, though, no serious work on Islamic history can afford to ignore alternative accounts of the Prophet's mission.

As Muslims feared, though, once you start removing the struts that support the tradition, someone might take a hammer to the whole structure. In *Crossroads to Islam* (2001), Yehuda Nevo (with Judith Koren) followed Crone in dismissing Muslim histories and relied solely on the scanty archaeological evidence we have from the Prophet's time. Finding that insufficient, he concluded that Muhammad never existed. We should not be surprised: it is a short leap from saying that the stories about the Prophet are fictional to saying the Prophet is a fictional figure.

But not all of Crone's intellectual descendants turned out to be radical sceptics, and at least one was interested in soberly cataloguing what evidence we do have of early Islam from non-Muslim sources. In 1997, Robert Hoyland, who had studied under Crone, published an astonishing sourcebook-cum-analysis called *Seeing Islam As Others Saw It*. Hoyland collected every reference to Islam – accidental or deliberate – in non-Muslim writings from the seventh and eighth centuries in languages from Syriac to Chinese. This volume deserves a place alongside the Qu'ran and Ibn Ishaq on any historian's shelf. Muslims, rather than dismissing Christian or Jewish chroniclers as hopelessly biased, might be surprised at how much they confirm the familiar narrative.

The *Doctrina Jacobi*, a Greek document written in 634, would almost certainly be forgotten today had it not mentioned in passing a disturbance in Palestine. Jacob, a convert to Christianity, is persuading a Jew named Justus to leave his religion. During their dispute, Justus says he has heard that some Arabs had recently killed a Roman guard. 'And they were saying,' he reports, 'that a prophet had appeared, coming with the Saracens, and that he was proclaiming the advent of the anointed one, the Christ who was to come.' Though he is not named this prophet is surely the Prophet. Here is firm contemporary evidence for the existence of Islam's founder that deflates Nevo's argument. There is only one problem: these attacks are supposed to have happened in 634, but the Prophet died in 632. Perhaps he did lead the Arabs into Palestine and the Muslims misremembered the date of his death; or perhaps the Jews who informed Justus had heard the Arabs proclaiming 'There is no god but God and Muhammad is his prophet', and mistook the general leading the troops for the Prophet. A more detailed account of the battle was provided by Thomas the Presbyter, writing in Syriac in 640: 'On Friday February 4 (634) there was a battle between the Romans and the Arabs of Muhammad in Palestine, 12 miles east of Gaza.' Here the Arabs are said to be followers of Muhammad – the first ever mention of his name – rather than being physically led by him. The report accords with later Muslim sources, which say a battle took place near Gaza in 634.

Hoyland pieces together a portrait of how outsiders saw the new believers during the first century: they were monotheist and iconoclastic; they reverenced a sanctuary associated with Abraham called 'the House of God' or the 'Ka'ba' towards which they prayed; a man named Muhammad was their 'guide' and 'instructor', whose laws they fiercely upheld; they were forbidden to eat carrion, drink wine or fornicate. This slots neatly into place with orthodox Islam. So rather than being a work-in-progress in its first 100 years, as argued by Crone and Holland, Islam seems to already have solid foundations.

Yet these records do raise an awkward question: why has more near-contemporary evidence about Muhammad survived from non-Muslims than from those who claimed to obsessively follow his commands? Even according to the orthodox view nothing was written down about the Prophet until seventy years after his death, and there are no definitive inscriptions bearing his name until the same time. The real question is not whether or not Muhammad existed – Crone's current position is that 'the evidence that a prophet was active among the Arabs in the early decades of the seventh century, on the eve of the Arab conquest of the Middle East, must be said to be exceptionally good' – but whether the early Muslims distorted his life beyond recognition to suit their theological or political ends, cobbling together ancient stories to create the Prophet's biography, rather as they used Byzantine models to build their mosques. The gap in the Muslim record allows revisionists to bolster this argument.

One solution means asking tough questions about Muslim veneration of Muhammad. Unlike Christianity, Islam has no divinely sanctioned Life of its founder – no equivalent to the Gospels. Indeed in the early days, it might have been actively hostile to making one. Muslims already had a book recording their founder's inspired utterances and a hagiography might have threatened the Qu'ran's supremacy. Arguably these suspicions proved to be well founded: from Ibn Ishaq onwards there proved a vast appetite for entertaining stories about the Prophet to supplement – and even supplant – the austere commands of the Qu'ran. This narrative yearning became more intense when the final companions – known in their time as the living tradition – began dying off. It is not a coincidence that at around the time when Muhammad's name was first appearing on coins, buildings and early written sources, the last person who could have claimed an acquaintance with him died in 693.

Another possible solution to the mystery of the absent Prophet lies in the archaeological record, a field that remained untouched until recently. Jeremy Johns, professor of Islamic archaeology at Oxford, has identified coins, papyri, building inscriptions, tombstones and travellers' graffiti with the Islamic invocation 'Bismillah', meaning 'In the name of God', dating to as early as 643 – eleven years after Muhammad's death. Some are marked with dates that run according to the Islamic calendar, calculated from when the Prophet moved from Mecca to Medina in 622. Yet very little else has survived until the 690s, and nothing until then that names Muhammad specifically.

Maybe Muslims were too busy sorting out what they believed before they set down the story. Or perhaps they were more interested in fighting one another for control of a burgeoning empire than in recording history they were still living. In any case the two kinds of object most likely to survive until the present day are coins and monumental buildings. For these to be created they need to be sponsored by a settled state – something Islam lacked until the caliph Abd al-Malik, who ruled from 685 to 705. 'The question to be answered,' says Johns, 'is not why proclamations of Islam are absent, but why media that carry such proclamations after 691–2 are so rare in the preceding period.' Memories fade and oral traditions can be distorted: for belief to flourish it needs to tell its story, which Abd al-Malik did most spectacularly in building the Dome of the Rock in Jerusalem, completed in 691.

THE PLACE

One major problem archaeology faces is that Saudi Arabia forbids excavation in Mecca and Medina. Our evidence for the cities' role in the rise of Islam is based on literary sources alone – and is therefore open to challenge by sceptics. The most controversial argument Tom Holland made in his documentary was that Mecca might not have been the place where Muhammad began his mission. To many viewers (Muslim and non-Muslim) the idea was too fanciful to credit. Mecca, the city towards which Muslims pray, appropriated by the English language as a metaphorical haven, is at the heart of Islam's story. Casting doubt on something so certain might seem wilfully provocative; but Holland had his reasons.

His argument originates mainly from Crone's *Meccan Trade and Rise of Islam* (1987), in which she took on contemporary academic orthodoxy about why Muhammad's religion flourished. Historians such as Montgomery Watt and Maxime Rodinson argued that Mecca's great trading riches created extreme inequalities of wealth. According to this narrative the Prophet's egalitarian message attracted followers excluded from the Meccan feast. But what exactly, Crone asked, was the commodity that made the city so rich? Roman historians do not mention Mecca and neither is it directly placed on the spice route from Yemen to Syria. 'What commodity was available in Arabia that could be transported at such a distance, through such an inhospitable environment, and still be sold at a profit large enough to support the growth of a city in a peripheral site bereft of natural resources?' she asked. Her answer was none.

But what if Mecca was not where we now think it is? Perhaps it *was* a rich trading centre, only positioned further north in Palestine – closer to the Byzantine Empire, after which a Qu'ranic chapter is named. As evidence, Crone quotes a verse about Lot's wife being turned into a pillar of salt. 'You pass by their ruins by day and by night' (37:138) warns the Qu'ran. The unfortunate lady's crystallised remains are in Palestine. How could the Meccans, she asks, who lived hundreds of miles away, be able to see them every morning and evening? Holland follows up this clue. He finds the multiple references to fertile land and fruits in the Qu'ran very odd in a book mostly revealed in barren Mecca. One chapter starts by swearing by the olive and fig – produce from Palestine, not Arabia. The two times Mecca is mentioned in the Qu'ran (one oddly calling it Becca) do not solve the problem, says Holland, because the location of the sacred sanctuary is never specified. The earliest mosques were inconsistent in their direction of prayer – some facing Jerusalem, some Mecca and some elsewhere. Could an alternative sanctuary have been suppressed by Islamic tradition? Or, as Crone suggested in 1987, perhaps there were two Meccas – one north and one south?

When Holland interviewed Crone for his documentary last year, she seemed rather coy about repeating her earlier theory, and refused to name an alternative to Mecca. In keeping with her habit of exploding received wisdom and then rowing back, Crone has revised her two Meccas theory. In a 2007 journal article, she proposed a commodity in which the Prophet's tribe might have traded. 'What the author of *Meccan Trade* did not know, 20 years ago,' she wrote, 'was that the Roman Army swallowed up colossal amounts of leather.' One legion needed 65,700 goat hides simply for tents. Mecca had pastoral regions and the Qu'ran describes cattle-skin tents that could easily be transported as 'God's bounty' (16:80). If Mecca got rich by exploiting the Byzantine wars with Persia, then being outside the Palestinian war zone would have been an advantage. 'For traders from the pastoralist regions, beyond the reach of the imperial taxation system, well away from the invasion routes and shielded by low population densities from the plague, the wars will have been a golden opportunity.' Which is as close as Crone comes to saying Mecca might well still be Mecca.

Holland's readings of the Qu'ran are not easy to confirm or refute. Yet the verse about the remains of Lot's wife being visible by day and night likely includes some rhetorical exaggeration, and rare fruits and crops are surely present for the same reason that water is important to a desert religion: scarcity breeds sanctity.

Also Holland omits to mention the verse of the Qu'ran (14:37) that says Abraham founded Mecca, 'in a valley where no vegetation grows, near your Sacred House'.

If the Arabs writing within sixty years of the Prophet's death did suppress the truth of an alternative location where Islam was really born, they left no trace of an argument. But non-Muslim sources play a part again in hinting at the religion's place of origin. Holland says the confusion over the direction of early mosques is evidence that the sacred house was not in Mecca. Whereas Jacob, Bishop of Edessa, writing between 684 and 688, noted that 'Muslims who are in Iraq pray to the west, towards the Ka'aba'. This supports the orthodox direction (south-west) though is still ambiguous. What about the mosques that irrefutably face away from the Ka'aba? In an invaluable discussion in *Seeing Islam*, Hoyland argues that Muslims might initially have taken over existing buildings and not fully converted them into mosques; and also – cockups always being more convincing than conspiracy in explaining human affairs – that they were pretty bad at calculating directions. Islamic graffiti dated to 660–61 has also been found around Mecca, which, he writes, 'would be inexplicable if Mecca was of little significance to the early Muslims'.

Should the alternative Mecca theory be consigned to the Dan Brown School of historical speculation? I believe yes – but it is still fascinating to see *why* Crone and Holland are determined to move Islam's birthplace from Arabia to near Jerusalem. We return once more to John Wansbrough, who in *The Sectarian Milieu* argued that a monotheistic religion such as Islam must have arisen from the debates between Jews and Christians in Palestine – not pagan Mecca. Reading the Qu'ran, it is certainly remarkable how often Biblical Prophets are invoked – Moses, Abraham, Solomon, Noah, Lot, Jesus. The stories have small variations from the Bible: Jesus, for example, is plucked from his crucifix and taken straight to Heaven. Could this be a remnant of the Christian Arian heresy supposedly snuffed out at the Council of Nicaea? And where might Muhammad have heard what the Meccans in the Qu'ran regarded as 'old fables'? By placing Muhammad near Jerusalem, Crone and Holland provide an answer that does not involve divine revelation.

Yet there are some hints in the tradition of Christian links to the Prophet. Ibn Ishaq tells us about Muhammad's trading journeys to Byzantine Syria where he met a monk called Bahira. There is also mention of Khadija's cousin, a Christian who knew scripture, and even a Gospel quotation on a Meccan stone. Might Muhammad have begun his mission somewhere more religiously diverse than is usually assumed? His target audience are described as *mushrikeen*, a word usually translated as 'idolaters' but which literally means 'sharers' – those who associate gods with God. These might be pagans or Christians who associate one of God's prophets with His son. Crone argues that the people listening to the Prophet's message were not idol worshippers but renegade monotheists. We need not go so far – Qu'ran 3:67 distinguishes clearly between Jews, Christians and *mushrikeen* – but it is true that understanding the audience that the Qu'ran was first created to address would help us to better unpack its message. Put another way, rather than taking Muhammad to the sectarian milieu, we could bring the sectarian milieu to Muhammad.

TWO MUHAMMADS

Two contrasting images offer partial portraits of the historical Muhammad – or at least how the earliest Muslims saw him. In 691, the caliph Abd al-Malik completed the Dome of the Rock, on which passages from the Qu'ran were openly proclaimed, along with Muhammad's prophethood and the name of a religion called 'Islam'. No one really knows why he built this magnificent sanctuary: one theory is that he wanted to set up a rival religious centre to Mecca, the base of a rival caliph over whom he had recently triumphed. This rival had also minted coins emblazoned with the Muslim phrase 'In the name of God'. In response, Abd al-Malik struck gold dinars with the witness statement 'There is no god but God, and Muhammad is His messenger', alongside the figure of a standing man.

The standing figure is usually designated as Abd al-Malik – that is how the British Museum labelled it when they displayed the coin in their 'History of the World in 100 Objects' exhibition. Robert Hoyland, though, has recently put forward an intriguing alternative view. The Byzantine Emperor Justinian II (685–95, 705–11) reacted to the threat of Islam by asserting his own Christian credentials. He put an effigy of Christ on his coins – the first time in history anyone had done so.

Justinian's Christ has flowing hair, a beard and no crown; Abd al-Malik's figure is shown with flowing hair, a beard and no crown. Could the caliph have been responding to the emperor's religious propaganda with an image not of himself but of the founder of his new religion? Could this be a portrait of the Prophet made almost within living memory of people who knew him? In his hand the figure carries what appears to be a scabbard with a sheathed sword. But Hoyland sees not a sword but a case with a scroll inside – the Qu'ran perhaps? His view is highly speculative (as he acknowledges) but if this is the Prophet then it tells us something about how this caliph wished him to be perceived. This is not Muhammad the spiritual leader or Muhammad the lawgiver: this is the Prophet armed, an embodiment of the victorious Arab general. The expression is implacably fierce and a whip hangs menacingly from his robes. Two generations after his death the caliphs were projecting their own self-image on to the Prophet and using his name – if perhaps not his direct image – to buttress their aggression.

A martial prophet might have inspired soldiers keen on accumulating gold dinars, but I doubt it did much for ordinary believers. For them a parallel process had begun: the elevation of Muhammad from human messenger to spiritual intercessor. A Dome of the Rock inscription pleads for Muhammad's help on the Day of Judgement – something impossible according to the Qu'ran, which says every person will account for his or her deeds without favour. Yet the people needed a prophet they could adore personally and who could be their saviour; in accommodating popular piety in such a public place, Abd al-Malik might have been acknowledging a growing trend to boost the Prophet's status.

Muhammad was also turned into a miracle-worker in the stories of Abd al-Malik's time. The Qu'ran explicitly says that while earlier prophets such as Moses were given wonders to perform, Muhammad was a 'plain warner' (29:50) made of flesh and blood (17:93). His miracle was the words he recited. But again this did not stop Muslims. One dramatic legend has Muhammad show the Meccans his divine access by splitting and then repairing the moon. The story originated in a passage from the Qu'ran describing the end of the world as when 'The Hour is at hand and the moon is split' (54:1). As Uri Rubin has carefully catalogued, this verse somehow transformed from an eschatological reference to a lunar eclipse to a literal moon splitting during the Prophet's mission. Like the Prophet's pulpit in Medina the story became embellished over time, and it features in many beautiful miniatures.

These two images of the Prophet – the general and the miracle worker – both have their origins in real history but were exaggerated by Muslims into rival visions. We can see the same divide today between the extremist Salafi and mystical Sufi strains of Islam. We cannot dismiss such quasi-historical documents: they are valuable records of how the Prophet was perceived by Muslims over the centuries.

By openly debating what we can and cannot reliably say about early Islam we will learn more about how the religion was created. This will not be an easy task for Muslims wedded to every detail of the traditional story; but it is necessary. In his lecture series *The Reconstruction of Religious Thought in Islam*, the Pakistani poet Muhammad Iqbal insisted on the need to ask discomfiting questions: 'Now since the transformation and guidance of man's inner and outer life is the essential aim of religion,' he said, 'it is obvious that the general truths which it embodies must not remain unsettled.' The revisionist scholars whose work I have touched on do not write in the hope of revivifying Islam; rather they see faith-claims as obstacles that need to be cleared away. But their work can be used by anyone who, like Iqbal, wishes new life to be breathed into a 1,400-year-old faith. For this Muslims need to be braver than the caliph who dared not touch the Prophet's pulpit. Western scholars are already removing the struts and supports that once held together the edifice of historical Islam. Only by learning from such approaches can the faithful challenge their wilder speculations, and stake a claim in how the pieces might be put back together.

– Note on Contributors –

MICHAEL IGNATIEFF teaches human rights and politics at the Kennedy School of Government, Harvard University and at the Munk School of Global Affairs, University of Toronto. He is the former leader of the Liberal Party of Canada and the author of fifteen works of fiction and non-fiction. His latest book is *Fire and Ashes: Success and Failure in Politics*.

J. T. BARBARESE has published five books of poetry and a translation of Euripides' *Children of Herakle*s (University of Pennsylvania Press, 1999). His poetry and translations have appeared in many journals and magazines, including the *Atlantic Monthly*, *Poetry*, *The New Yorker* and the *Times Literary Supplement*; his fiction in *Boulevard*, *NAR*, and, prior to becoming its editor in 2008, in,*StoryQuarterly*; and his literary journalism in *Poetry*, *The Sewanee Review*, *The New York Times*, and *The Columbia History of American Poetry*. He is presently Senior Editor of *StoryQuarterly*.

BELLE BOGGS is the author of *Mattaponi Queen*, a collection of linked stories, and the forthcoming novel *The Ugly Bear List*, both from Graywolf Press. *Mattaponi Queen* won the Bakeless Prize and the Emyl Jenkins Sexton Literary Award from the Library of Virginia, and was shortlisted for the Frank O'Connor International Short Story Award. Her work has appeared in *Orion*, *Harper's*, *The Paris Review*, *Slate*, *The Sun*, and *The New New South*, among other publications.

LESLIE JAMISON was born in Washington DC and raised in Los Angeles. She is a graduate of Harvard College and the Iowa Writers' Workshop. Her work has appeared or is forthcoming in publications including *Harper's*, *The New York Times*, *The Believer*, and *Oxford American*. Her first novel, *The Gin Closet*, was a finalist for the LA Times First Fiction Award, and her second book, a collection of essays called *The Empathy Exams*, won the Graywolf Press Nonfiction Prize and will be published by Graywolf and Granta UK in 2014.

ANDREW O'HAGAN was born in Glasgow in 1968. He wrote *The Missing* and four novels, two of which were nominated for the Booker Prize, as well as a book of essays, *The Atlantic Ocean*. He writes for the *London Review of Books* and *The New York Times*.

SAMEER RAHIM is Assistant Books Editor at the *Telegraph*.

nh Notting Hill Editions

Notting Hill Editions is devoted to the best in essay writing. Our authors, living and dead, cover a broad range of non-fiction, but all display the virtues of brevity, soul and wit.

To discover more, please visit www.nottinghilleditions.com